THE POLITICS OF PARADISE

Frank Field has been Member of Parliament for Birkenhead since 1979. From 1969 to 1979 he was Director of the Child Poverty Action Group. In 1974 he formed the Low Pay Unit. He is an Anglican.

Books by Frank Field

As author
Unequal Britain (1974)
Inequality In Britain: Freedom, Welfare And The State (1981)
Poverty And Politics (1982)
The Minimum Wage: Its Potential And Dangers (1984)
Freedom And Wealth In A Socialist Future (1987)

As Co-author
To Him Who Hath: A Study Of Poverty And Taxation (1976)

As Editor
20th Century State Education (jointly) (1971)
Black Britons (jointly) (1971)
Low Pay (1973)
Are Low Wages Inevitable? (1976)
Education And The Urban Crisis (1976)
The Conscript Army: A Study Of Britain's Unemployed (1976)
The Wealth Report 1 (1979)
The Wealth Report 2 (1983)
Policies Against Low Pay: An International Perspective
(PSI, 1984)

Frank Field

THE POLITICS
OF PARADISE

A Christian Approach
To The Kingdom

Collins
FOUNT PAPERBACKS

First published in Great Britain in 1987 by
Fount Paperbacks, London

Copyright © Frank Field 1987

Made and printed in Great Britain by
William Collins Sons & Co. Ltd, Glasgow

To Nan, my mother,
whose life is an example of
living the Kingdom

O world invisible, we view thee,
O world intangible, we touch thee,
O world unknowable, we know thee,
Inapprehensible, we clutch thee.

Francis Thompson

("The Kingdom Of God", *The Poems of Francis Thompson,*
Hollis & Carter, 1946, p.199)

Acknowledgements

The author acknowledges with gratitude his debt to the works of other writers, all of which are fully acknowledged either in the text itself or in the Notes.

In those cases where extensive quotation has been made he is grateful to the copyright-holders for permission to use their material.

Contents

Preface

There are a number of people who have helped with the writing of this book, and I wish to thank them. Kay Andrews, as usual, patiently debated with me as I tried to clarify my ideas. Bob Clements read and commented on Chapter One, and Monsignor John McDonald checked a number of the biblical references. The Reverend Perry Butler spent time with me talking over the ideas which have found their way into Chapter Six. Mehru Azim, Dora Clark and Aileen Muir, of the House of Commons Library, traced numerous publications for me, some of which have been included in the text of this book. I also wish to thank the trustees of the Rowntree Social Service Trust, which awarded me a small grant to cover the cost of preparing the manuscript.

Two other people, who are particularly important to me, have played a major part in producing this volume. This book was begun during those dark days, when my reselection process in Birkenhead was slowly wending its way to a conclusion. My secretary, Joan Hammell, not only cheered me through that dreadful experience, which covered a number of years, and coped with all the secretarial side of my parliamentary work, but also found time to type the drafts of this work. My continuing debt to her is considerable. I am indebted too, to Damian Leeson, who is my personal assistant. Damian has edited the manuscript for the press and, in so doing, has made me argue sections more clearly. The book now bears something of his writing abilities. Despite his, and Joan's, skills, I alone am responsible for any errors which remain, as well as for the opinions expressed in the following pages.

Frank Field,
Birkenhead, January 1987

1.

The Old Testament Kingdom

The phrase "The Kingdom of God" or "The Kingdom of heaven" is almost as old as the Jewish religion itself. This chapter, while looking at how the idea was presented to the Jewish people by the Old Testament prophets, suggests that the Kingdom was never presented as a single vision. While there was no debate about where the Kingdom was to be located – the prophets agreed that it was to have earthly roots – there was disagreement as to how the New Jerusalem was to be built. There are those Old Testament prophets who saw its establishment in terms of the spread of social righteousness, while others emphasized personal piety. Both these traditions are however compatible, sharing a belief that, through God's grace, a frail nation would be transformed into an ideal society.

There were differences too about how quickly the Kingdom was to be established. For most of the period covered by the Old Testament, this process is viewed as a gradual one, although, towards the end of the Old Testament record, at a time when the Israelite nation was again subject to foreign domination, it was widely believed that the Kingdom would soon be established through Yahweh's direct intervention.

A Homeland

For convenience, I propose a somewhat artificial subdivision of the Old Testament into four distinct historical periods. The first covers the nomadic period following the conquest of Canaan and prior to the emergence of the canonical prophets. At its inception, the "nation" was, in reality, no more than a collection of migratory tribes. The poverty endemic to such a nomadic existence created

13

bonds of loyalty necessary to the survival of the tribe. As we shall see, the feeling of duty to one's fellow tribesman featured prominently in the teaching of the prophets, although by that stage the loyalty extended beyond the narrow confines of the tribe itself.

Throughout recorded history, and no doubt before, mankind has expressed a need to worship gods. To this general rule the Jewish people were no exception. They too were ready to try to win the favour of their God, or, alternatively, to assuage His wrath, by offering sacrifices. Slowly, however, a more distinctive tradition emerges, as the Jewish people come to believe that Jehova has entered into a special relationship, a personal and unique covenant with them.

In Genesis there are two accounts of this covenant being struck.[1] In the second we learn that the covenant made between God and Abraham encompasses Abraham's descendants, and promises that they shall be masters of the land in which he is, at present, a nomad.

> Behold, my covenant is with you, and you shall be the father of a multitude of nations. No longer shall your name be Abram, but your name shall be Abraham, for I have made you the father of a multitude of nations. I will make you exceedingly fruitful; and I will make nations of you, and kings shall come forth from you. And I will establish my covenant between me and you and your descendants after you throughout their generations for an everlasting covenant, to be God to you and your descendants after you. And I will give to you and your descendants after you, the land of your sojournings, all the land of Canaan for an everlasting possession; and I will be their God.[2]

Abraham cannot believe that his aged and barren wife Sarah will produce any children, and laughingly refers God to the son he has had by Hagar. But this son is not the heir to the covenant. The true son and heir, as yet unborn, is named by God as Isaac, meaning "he laughs". And so the mystery of the covenant begins to unfold.

The conquest of Canaan marks the period prior to the emergence of the canonical prophets. The conquest itself was of great significance to the emergence of Israel, although it did not, in itself, prevent Israel from being attacked by rebel Canaanites, surrounding tribes and, of course, the Philistines. The establishment of a monarchy did afford some protection from surrounding enemies. However, the monarchy and its forces had somehow to be financed, and this raised the perennial question as to who should and who should not pay taxes.

The conquest led also to the gradual replacement of the nation's traditional nomadic existence by a settled, yeoman-based, agrarian economy. The family, and loyalty to it, replaced loyalty to the tribe. The family itself was viewed as a land-holding unit.

It is also during this period that there emerges the concept of the land constituting an inalienable gift of God, an aspect of the covenant He has entered into with His Chosen People. It is this belief which underlies the Old and New Testament approach to wealth. The belief that land constituted a divine gift led the Israelites to view ownership, not in absolute terms, but rather as a trusteeship, limiting the power of the owner to do what he would with it.

This notion of trusteeship, as opposed to ownership, is demonstrated in Kings, when Ahab, the Israelite king, wishing to extend his palace garden, asks Naboth, the owner of a neighbouring vineyard, for his property.

> "Give me your vineyard, that I may have it for a vegetable garden, because it is near my house; and I will give you a better vineyard for it; or, if it seems good to you, I will give you its value in money."[3]

Naboth, however, refuses the offer, stating:

> "The Lord forbid that I should give you the inheritance of my fathers."[4]

In order to acquire the vineyard, Ahab's wife, Jezebel, writes letters, in her husband's name, to the elders and nobles of the city, as part of her plot against Naboth. Jezebel requests the elders to:

"Proclaim a fast, and set Naboth on high among the people; and set two base fellows opposite him, and let them bring a charge against him, saying, 'You have cursed God and the king'. Then take him out and stone him to death." And the men of his city . . . did as Jezebel had sent word to them.[5]

This action prompted the fiercest of denunciations from Elijah, and led ultimately to Ahab losing his throne and Jezebel her life.

The Kingdom Asserted

It is during the later stage of this first period that changes in the economy led to a break-up of the old system of land ownership. This appears to have been quickly exploited by the rich, and it is against this backdrop that the canonical prophets, Amos, Hosea, Isaiah and Micah, emerge and call for a restoration of the old property rights. Their message is not, however, confined merely to a condemnation of the powerful. What they have to say also has a profound effect on what is seen as proper conduct, and indeed helps shape an entire concept of morality. There is, consequently, a decisive shift, away from an emphasis on sacrificial presentations aimed at appeasing God, to an exclusive concern with personal behaviour designed to please Him. This tone of moral judgement is discernible in Micah, where we read:

> "Woe to those who devise wickedness
> and work evil upon their beds!
> When the morning dawns, they perform it,
> because it is in the power of their hand.
> They covet fields, and seize them;
> and houses, and take them away;
> they oppress a man and his house,
> a man and his inheritance."[6]

Micah continues to condemn the powerful "who hate the good and love the evil", warning his listeners of divine judgement.[7]

"Hear this, you heads of the house of Jacob
and rulers of the house of Israel,
who abhor justice and pervert all equity,
who build Zion with blood
and Jerusalem with wrong.
Its heads give judgement for a bribe,
its priests teach for hire,
its prophets divine for money."[8]

For this:

"Zion shall be ploughed as a field;
Jerusalem shall become a heap of ruins,
and the mountain of the house a wooded height."[9]

Condemnation of those who oppress the weak is a constant theme.
Isaiah echoes Micah's concern, warning:

"Woe to those who decree iniquitous decrees,
and the writers who keep writing oppression,
to turn aside the needy from justice
and to rob the poor of my people of their right,
that widows may be their spoil,
and that they may make the fatherless their prey!"[10]

The divine displeasure, incurred by such acts, could not, so the
prophets taught, be assuaged simply by offering sacrifices. God
demands a change in the form of worship, away from ritualized
offerings which, alone, mean nothing, to a recognition of individual
rights and justice.

"What to me is the multitude of your sacrifices?
    says the Lord;
I have had enough of burnt offerings of rams
    and the fat of fed beasts;

I do not delight in the blood of bulls,
 or of lambs, or of he-goats.
When you come to appear before me,
 who requires of you
 this trampling of my courts?
Bring no more vain offerings;
 incense is an abomination to me."[11]

Without proper conduct such acts are hollow and achieve nothing.

"When you spread forth your hands,
 I will hide my eyes from you;
even though you make many prayers,
 I will not listen;
your hands are full of blood.
Wash yourselves; make yourselves clean;
 remove the evil of your doings from before my eyes."[12]

Instead of offering sacrifice, the commandment is to:

"Cease to do evil,
Learn to do good;
Seek justice,
Correct oppression;
Defend the fatherless,
Plead for the widow."[13]

Isaiah presents us with an unmistakable image of God as the redresser of wrongs, protector of the poor and the oppressed, husband to the widow and father to the orphan.

Micah is in complete harmony with Isaiah, emphasizing again that God demands righteous behaviour and not ritual sacrifice.

"He has showed you, O man, what is good;
 and what does the Lord require of you

but to do justice, and to love kindness,
and to walk humbly with your God?"[14]

There are then two powerful themes inherent in the teaching of the canonical prophets. The plea for justice for the poor and the oppressed is inextricably linked to the notion that this is to be achieved as part of man's worship of God. Correct religious practice is viewed in terms of behaviour rather than ritual. Such behaviour is presented by the prophets as the true way to build the New Jerusalem or the Kingdom.

In another passage, Isaiah not only lists what constitutes righteous behaviour, but links this conduct to the qualities of the individual who will lead Israel towards that ideal earthly Kingdom.

"There shall come forth a shoot from the stump of Jesse,
 and a branch shall grow out of his roots.
And the Spirit of the Lord shall rest upon him,
 the spirit of wisdom and understanding,
 the spirit of counsel and might,
 the spirit of knowledge and the fear of the Lord.
And his delight shall be in the fear of the Lord.
He shall not judge by what his eyes see,
 or decide by what his ears hear;
but with righteousness he shall judge the poor,
 and decide with equity for the meek of the earth;
and he shall smite the earth with the rod of his mouth,
 and with the breath of his lips he shall slay the wicked.
Righteousness shall be the girdle of his waist,
 and faithfulness the girdle of his loins . . .
In that day the root of Jesse shall stand as an ensign to the
 peoples;
him shall the nations seek, and his dwelling shall be
 glorious . . ."[15]

The Rise of Private Religion

The third stage of Israel's Old Testament development encompasses the last days of the monarchy, when the country was under attack, and the subsequent period of exile. During Isaiah's lifetime the northern kingdom fell to the Assyrians, and Judah was subjected to Babylonian and Assyrian incursions. Within a century and a half of the fall of the northern kingdom, Judah fell to Nebuchadnezzar.

During the previous period of Israel's history, prophecy had concentrated on the nation, its future and well-being. The collapse of the state naturally had a profound effect upon the prophetic message. How could there be an appeal to national righteousness when the nation no longer existed?

Religion had to become personal in order to survive. Private prayer and devotion were the only safe religious activities for an individual ruled by a foreign power. Thus, it is during this period that we witness a birth of religious individualism. This move towards individual piety, a formerly unexplored dimension of religious experience, is first discernible in Jeremiah.

Commenting on this trend, Walter Rauschenbusch has noted how:

> "the subtlest springs of human personality were liberated when the individual realized that he personally was dear to God and could work out his salvation, not as a member of a nation, but as a man by virtue of his humanity."[16]

There were, however, dangers implicit in this trend. For all too many, this change in religious activity was thought of as a pure gain, rather than a development forced by circumstance. Instead of creating a synthesis of the two traditions, the new and the old, the move towards personal holiness was emphasized, by priest and teacher alike, at the expense of the older tradition.

Though this was the dominant trend, a plurality of views about the role of religion was none the less maintained. The prophets, during the exile, were principally concerned with the restoration of the nation and:

"insisted on personal holiness, not because that was the end of all religion, but because it was the condition and guarantee of national restoration."[17]

Yet, despite the emphasis on personal piety, the older prophetic tradition was not totally silent. Ezekiel, for example, spoke of the righteous man as one who:

" . . . does not oppress anyone, but restores to the debtor his pledge, commits no robbery, gives his bread to the hungry and covers the naked with a garment, does not lend at interest or take any increase, withholds his hand from iniquity, executes true justice between man and man, walks in my statutes, and is careful to observe my ordinances – he is righteous, he shall surely live, says the Lord God."[18]

Likewise, in part of Jeremiah's prophecy, we can detect support for the traditional system of land tenure.[19] Immediately prior to the fall of Jerusalem, Jeremiah exercised the right of proscription to enable a family to retain its property.

Jeremiah said, "The word of the Lord came to me: Behold, Hanamel the son of Shallum your uncle will come to you and say, 'Buy my field which is at Anathoth, for the right of redemption by purchase is yours.' Then Hanamal my cousin came to me in the court of the guard, in accordance with the word of the Lord, and said to me, 'Buy my field which is at Anathoth in the land of Benjamin, for the right of possession and redemption is yours; buy it for yourself.' Then I knew that this was the word of the Lord."[20]

The cynical manumission of slaves, according to the terms of the Jubilee, by King Zedekiah, princes and slave owners when the Chaldeans were besieging Jerusalem, only to reimpose slavery when it appeared that the threat of being overrun had been averted, likewise aroused Jeremiah's wrath, and, according to him, made the captivity inevitable.

> The word of the Lord came to Jeremiah from the Lord: "Thus says the Lord, the God of Israel: I made a covenant with your fathers when I brought them out of the land of Egypt, out of the house of bondage, saying, 'At the end of six years each of you must set free the fellow Hebrew who has been sold to you and has served you six years; you must set him free from your service.' But your fathers did not listen to me or incline their ears to me. You recently repented and did what was right in my eyes by proclaiming liberty, each to his neighbour, and you made a covenant before me in the house which is called by my name; but then you turned around and profaned my name when each of you took back his male and female slaves, whom you had set free according to their desire, and you brought them into subjection to be your slaves. Therefore, thus says the Lord: You have not obeyed me by proclaiming liberty, every one to his brother and to his neighbour; behold, I proclaim to you liberty to the sword, to pestilence, and to famine, says the Lord. I will make you a horror to all the kingdoms of the earth."[21]

This abuse of the Jubilee laws does none the less demonstrate their continued existence and importance. Therefore, despite an emphasis on personal holiness, a number of old established laws, relating to the loss of land and the rights of the poor, continued to be asserted. These laws guaranteed the right to eat a portion of the produce while crossing a vineyard or cornfield, the right to a portion of any olive harvest, and the right for resident aliens, orphans and widows to enjoy the hospitality of the rich during festive occasions. There were also laws prohibiting overworking and ensuring the prompt payment of wages. Such directions were not confined solely to the relief of pauperism. Others, as we have just seen, struck at landlessness, the very root of poverty. These rules ranged from the release of slaves every six years and the cancellation of all debts after a seven-year period, to the return of all land, after a fifty-year period, to its original owner. The continual denunciation, by the prophets, of those individuals who disregarded such laws suggests that they remained more an ideal than a practical reality. None the less, they are indicative of the moral objectives of Jewish society at that time.

Important as this re-emphasis of the older collective values is, what is distinctive about this third stage of Israel's development is the new dimension to religious experience, to ideas about the nature of the Kingdom and the historical roots for that part of Christianity which stresses, above all else, the need for personal holiness. It is equally important to bear in mind the forces which brought this tradition into being. Not surprisingly, the possibility of creating an ideal state faded into the background during the period of foreign domination. Instead of emphasizing the importance of the Jewish state, the religious leaders understandably became obsessed with building what was, in effect, a Jewish Church. This was a period when the priest grew in importance and, while the ideal city is still seen as a city of righteousness, it is a righteousness which stems, not from justice, but from true worship. The message of the older prophets, the condemnation of man's injustice and the oppression of his fellow man, is overshadowed by a new emphasis on man's personal sin against God. To assuage His wrath, the more primitive Israelite emphasis on sacrificial and ceremonial practice once again comes to the fore.

Building a Jewish Church

The fourth period of Israel's history, as recorded in the Old Testament, occurs immediately after the exile. However, the return of the Jews from Babylon did not amount to a restoration of the old order and an independent Jewish state. Some home rule was granted, but the Jews around Jerusalem were subject to non-Jewish powers throughout the remainder of the Old Testament record, and indeed beyond. While such circumstances made it impossible for the prophets to begin to propose, once again, the foundation of an ideal state, the longing for its establishment was none the less continuously present. This very aspiration can be seen, for example, in the use of prayer in the synagogues at the time of Jesus. The prayer, which calls for the establishment of the Kingdom during the lifetime of the supplicant, contains the following plea:

> "Magnified and sanctified be His great name in the world which He has created according to His will. May He establish His Kingdom in your lifetime and in your days, in the lifetime of the House of Israel, even speedily and at a near time."[22]

But, whereas in previous periods the prophets had seen its establishment occurring as part of an inevitable progression towards that ideal, now, in this period, prophecy focused on the establishment of the ideal state through divine intervention. As one commentator has observed:

> "The new Israel was no longer to be looked for through the adaptation and transformation of an independent state and natural existence; but the new Jerusalem was come down from God out of heaven."[23]

Despite this changing conception about how the ideal state would emerge, the prophetic spirit was not totally silent on the question of social righteousness at this time. Significantly, after the return from exile, land was distributed according to the ancient custom, as Joshua recounted in his description of the division of Palestine among the tribes of Israel as prescribed by divine revelation.

> "Their inheritance was by lot, as the Lord had commanded Moses for the nine and one-half tribes. For Moses had given an inheritance to the two and one-half tribes beyond the Jordan; but to the Levites he gave no inheritance among them. For the people of Joseph were two tribes, Manasseh and Ephraim; and no portion was given to the Levites in the land, but only cities to dwell in, with their pasture lands for their cattle and their

24

substance. The people of Israel did as the Lord commanded Moses; they alloted the land."[24]

Likewise, the law attempted, as in previous times, to prevent families losing their landed possessions. Heavy taxation, together with bad harvests, resulted in a considerable number of farmers falling into debt. The closure of these mortgages resulted, as before, in the acquisition of large estates by the wealthy money-lenders. At one stage the landless peasants appealed to Nehemiah, whose moral suasion had so little effect on the landowners that he called together the whole Jewish nation, winning an agreement to cease interest payments and restore land to its original owners. Profiting from the earlier example of Zedekiah who, as we have seen, reneged on his commitments once the threat had passed, Nehemiah successfully enforced the agreement by means of a solemn oath.

"And I called the priests, and took an oath of them to do as they had promised. I also shook out my lap and said, 'So may God shake every man from his house and from his labour who does not perform this promise. So may he be shaken and emptied.' And all the assembly said 'Amen' and praised the Lord. And the people did as they had promised."[25]

Conclusion

The concept of the Kingdom grew and developed throughout the Old Testament. Initially, the Jews attempted to appease their God by means of sacrifice, a common enough practice among most races at that time. Gradually, however, the Jews came to believe that they enjoyed a special relationship, or covenant, with God, and the idea of appeasing Him through sacrificial actions was replaced by the emphasis which the prophets placed on righteous behaviour and actions. Salvation was seen exclusively as a collective rather than an individual act and, by this collective action, society was to be transformed into an ideal state. Essential to this development was the concept of righteousness, or right conduct, which was now defined in terms of justice for the oppressed.

The Jewish conception of the Kingdom was radically transformed during the later monarchical period and the ensuing period, known as the exile. Whereas previously their ideas had centred on an existing state being moulded into an ideal one, now, with the nation state in ruins, the Jews began to develop the idea of what amounted to the establishment of a Jewish Church. This period also witnessed a major shift in emphasis, away from a state of righteousness, achieved through a combination of personal and collective actions, to a vision of a righteous state as one concerned with the minutiae of ceremonial worship. Despite this change, the Jews, throughout the Old Testament, still looked to the establishment of the Kingdom in this world. There is however a significant change, as the Jews began to believe that this Kingdom would not come about by evolutionary means, but rather by the direct intervention of God. It is against this background of Jewish beliefs about the Kingdom that one needs to consider one of the central messages of the Gospel.

2.

Phrase with a History

How then was the term "Kingdom of heaven" or "Kingdom of God" used by Jesus? These phrases appear fourteen times in Mark's record, and there are thirty-two such citations in Luke. In Matthew, while the term "the Kingdom of God" makes only four appearances, the phrase, "the Kingdom of heaven" is referred to in no less than thirty-three places.[1] These phrases are, however, used in a number of ways and would appear to denote three different stages of development: the imminence of the Kingdom, the establishment and growth of the Kingdom in the world, and the completion of the Kingdom at the Second Coming. How do the Synoptic Gospels describe these three stages of the Kingdom's development?

The Kingdom at Hand

Let us consider, first of all, how the Kingdom was announced. In Matthew's Gospel we find John the Baptist preaching in the wilderness and saying:

"Repent, the Kingdom of heaven is at hand."[2]

Matthew also attributes a similar saying to Jesus after John has baptized Him, and after Jesus has fasted and been tempted in the wilderness.

From that time Jesus began to preach, saying: "Repent, for the Kingdom of heaven is at hand."[3]

27

Mark opens his narrative with a similar record of events.

Now after John was arrested, Jesus came into Galilee, preaching the Gospel of God, and saying, "The time is fulfilled and the Kingdom of God is at hand; repent and believe in the gospel."[4]

Matthew also writes of Jesus going about Galilee, teaching in the synagogues and preaching the Gospel of the Kingdom, while at the same time healing every disease and infirmity among the people.

At other junctures in the gospel story, Jesus is reported as proclaiming the imminence of the Kingdom of God. In Luke we learn of seventy other disciples being appointed to go ahead to tell the inhabitants of those towns which Jesus intended visiting that:

"The Kingdom of God has come near to you."[5]

By recording "the time is fulfilled", Mark links Jesus to the prophecies of Isaiah, as recorded in Chapter One, emphasizing that His Coming is that of the long-awaited Messiah. But His Messiahship was not one which gained acceptance among the Jews. This Messiahship, as proclaimed by Jesus, was inextricably bound up with His preaching of the Kingdom, and the nature of this Kingdom begins to unfold in the record of the temptations in the desert. Here Jesus emphasizes that He is not promoting secular Messianism, although for many Jews this was precisely what was expected and wanted. Instead Jesus rejects the "offer" of all the Kingdoms of the world.

And the devil took him up, and showed him all the kingdoms of the world in a moment of time, and said to him, "To you I will give all this authority and their glory; for it has been delivered to me, and I give it to whom I will. If you, then, will worship me, it shall all be yours." And Jesus answered him, "It is written, 'You shall worship the Lord your God, and him only shall you serve'."[6]

Notice too how the proclamation of the Kingdom is accompanied by the performing of miracles. Mark records Jesus' first miracle as taking place in the Capernaum synagogue, where He drives out an unclean spirit from one of the company.[7]

Luke also records the same event as Jesus' first miracle,[8] while Matthew's more general account is of Jesus passing into Galilee:

> preaching the Gospel of the Kingdom and healing every disease and every infirmity among the people.[9]

Here, surely, the miracles symbolize God's power entering the world in a new form. This power is one which directly confronts and vanquishes evil, often portrayed as an unclean spirit.

The Kingdom Growing

The performance of miracles leads us directly on to the second way in which Jesus refers to the Kingdom. He not only speaks of the Kingdom but suggests that His Coming has initiated the process of extending it. This is the underlying meaning of the Parables of Growth. On a number of occasions Jesus poses the question:

> "What is the Kingdom of God like? And to what shall I compare it? It is like a grain of mustard seed which a man took and sowed in his garden; and it grew and became a tree, and the birds of the air made nests in its branches."[10]

It was a misconception, popularly held at that time, that the mustard seed was the smallest of seeds.[11] Yet, the symbolism inherent in the growth of that seed into a large tree would not therefore be lost on Jesus' audience. The tree is the image of God's Kingdom and the reference to the resting place for birds of the air is presumably an echo of Daniel's comparison between God's Kingdom and that of Nebuchadnezzar, whose empire incorporated the whole world and all its people.

Later in Luke, Jesus compares the Kingdom to:

leaven which a woman took and hid in three measures of flour, till it was all leavened.[12]

Leaven is rarely mentioned in the New Testament, and when it is, it is used as a symbol for good. Here, the leaven represents the irreversible growth of the Kingdom from small beginnings. Matthew has it devouring three measures of meal, which is clearly an exaggeration.

Matthew records both parables.[13] Mark records the parable of the mustard seed, adding:

it is the smallest of all the seeds on earth; yet when it is sown it grows up and becomes the greatest of all shrubs, and puts forth large branches, so that the birds of the air can make nests in its shade.[14]

Another sowing parable likewise emphasizes the contrast between what appears to be a modest beginning to the Kingdom and the ultimate harvest. The sower sows, and some of the seed falls along the path and the birds come and devour it. Other seed falls on rough ground, where, the soil being shallow and poor, it cannot take root, is scorched by the sun, withers and dies. Other seed falls among thorns and the thorns grow up and choke it, and it yields no grain. Yet more seed falls on good ground and brings forth grain, yielding thirtyfold and sixtyfold and a hundredfold. A ratio of one to twenty would have been considered a remarkable harvest. So, despite the fact that much of the grain fell upon three types of soil and was lost, the harvest is none the less an unexpected bonanza. So too with the Kingdom of God: while the beginning may appear small and even discouraging, the growth into an unexpectedly plentiful harvest is assured.

To what extent is the Kingdom established? Some theologians have challenged the threefold development of the Kingdom at hand, the Kingdom growing and the Kingdom completed, as presented here. In the early 1930s, the biblical scholar, C.H. Dodd, published a little classic entitled *The Parables of the Kingdom*. In this he expressed the following view about the establishment of the Kingdom.

"Something has happened", Dodd writes of the early ministry of Jesus, "which has not happened before, and which means that the sovereign power of God has come into effective operation. It is not a matter of having God for your king in the sense that you obey His commandments: it is a matter of being confronted with the power of God at work in the world. In other words, the eschatological 'Kingdom of God is proclaimed as a present fact, which men must recognize, whether by their actions they accept or reject it.'"[15]

One of the key phrases here is Dodd's reference to the eschatological Kingdom of God; in other words the establishment of the Kingdom as part of the last events in historical time. Dodd, maintaining that we are in the eschatological period, argues that the Kingdom is not only firmly established, but established so completely that there is no other event concerning the Kingdom which will occur before the end of time.

In a later work he writes of the total impression given in the gospels that the forecasts of the Coming of the Kingdom in history (fulfilled in the resurrection of Jesus) are balanced by forecasts of a Coming beyond history:

". . . definitely, I should say, beyond history, and not as a further action in history, not even in the last event."[16]

This view of the Kingdom as already fully established is untenable on a number of counts. If what Dodd claims is in fact true, Christians are clearly left in some kind of limbo.[17] If the Kingdom is already established, what role do we have on this earth? We certainly don't have a political one. Moreover, we know from our own experiences and senses that the Kingdom is not yet established in any full or total sense. While many God-like actions are performed, there are similarly countless acts of evil being perpetrated.

Dodd's view also conflicts with the total record in the Scriptures, where there are a whole range of promises about the Kingdom. Reflecting on these, Charles Gore noted seven prophecies, where the Kingdom of God:

* Is looked upon as being the reign of God in a purified Israel.

* Is sometimes seen by the prophets to involve the kingship of the House of David.

* Involves a Christ figure made man, upon whom there would be an outpouring of the Holy Spirit.

* Would be accompanied by a new covenant given by God, which would be of greater significance than the covenant made through Moses.

* Will not be established by force of arms, but rather by the exercise of the virtues of meekness and suffering even unto death.

* Once established, will involve the overthrow of all Godless tyrannies.

* Involves a Second Coming of the Son of God, which will signify the end of history.[18]

Looking at these seven prophecies about the Coming of the Kingdom, it is apparent that only five have been fulfilled. The last two in Gore's list – the overthrow of all Godless tyrannies and the Second Coming, which will signify the end of history – await fulfilment.

32

One of the Parables of Growth links the idea of the Kingdom initiated, but in no way completed, with the hope of its full establishment at the Second Coming. Matthew records the Kingdom of heaven as being like a man who sowed good seed in his field but, while he was sleeping, his enemy came and sowed weeds among the wheat. The master, when he realized what had happened, instructed that the weeds were to be left, "lest in gathering the weeds you root up the wheat along with them".[19] At the harvest the weeds will be gathered first and burnt, while the wheat will be gathered into the barn.

The disciples asked Jesus to explain this parable, which He does in the following way. The good and the wicked are allowed to co-exist, until harvest time. Then, just as the weeds are gathered and burned, so shall it be at the end of time, when the Son of Man will send His angels and they will gather out of His Kingdom all causes of sin and all evildoers. Then the righteous will live like the Son in the Kingdom of the Father.

This argument in no way detracts from the central point of Dodd's message. Dodd is undoubtedly correct in assuming that, through the Incarnation, God has intervened in a direct way, and that this event marks a fundamental turning point in history. However, the New Testament record suggests that this event, though unprecedented and of inestimable importance, marks the initiation rather than the completion of the Kingdom. This completion is envisaged as a separate stage of development, and it is to this third and final stage that we now turn our attention.

The Completion of the Kingdom

There are a number of references in the New Testament to the Second Coming, as distinct to the Coming of the Spirit at Pentecost. Of all the Evangelists, Mark is the most succinct in his description.

"And then they will see the Son of Man coming on clouds with great power and glory."[20]

Luke too refers to the Second Coming.

> "For whoever is ashamed of me and of my words, of him will the Son of man be ashamed when He comes with glory and the glory of the Father and the holy angels."[21]

The timing of the Second Coming, according to Mark, is known to the Father alone.

> "But of that day or that hour no one knows, not even the angels in heaven, nor the Son, but only the Father."[22]

Luke gives a fuller description of the Second Coming.

> "And there will be signs in sun and moon and stars, and upon the earth distress of nations in perplexity at the roaring of the sea and of the waves, men fainting with fear and with foreboding of what is coming in the world; for the powers of heaven will be shaken. And then they will see the Son of man coming on a cloud with power and great glory. Now when these things begin to take place, look up and raise your hands, because your redemption is drawing near."[23]

In Luke's account, Jesus explains these events in parable form.

> "Look at the fig tree, and all the trees; and as soon as they come out in leaf, you see for yourselves and know that the summer is already near. So also, when you see these things taking place, you know the Kingdom of God is near."[24]

Scriptures also suggest that this third stage in the development of the Kingdom should itself be considered in two stages: first of all the reign on earth and then the establishment, beyond history, of the Kingdom. However, this distinction is not one which directly concerns us here. Instead, attention should be paid to the *second* stage, to the Kingdom which, though present and growing, is none the less incomplete. How is this Kingdom described in the New Testament?

A Gift

At one point, Jesus warns his disciples not to be unduly concerned with the trivia of this life. He tells the twelve:

"Do not seek what you are to eat and what you are to drink, nor be of anxious mind . . . (for) . . . your Father knows you need them."[25]

The disciples are instead invited to:

"seek His Kingdom, and these things shall be yours as well".[26]

The Kingdom, it is stressed, is not of man's creation. Rather:

"It is your Father's good pleasure to give you the Kingdom."[27]

While the Kingdom is treated as a gift, it is presented as no ordinary one. It is, rather, a gift which should be prized above all others and, as such, it is beyond price. This is illustrated in Matthew, where Jesus compares the Kingdom of heaven to a merchant in search of fine pearls who:

"on finding one pearl of great value, went and sold all that he had and bought it."[28]

And again, it is compared to:

"a treasure hidden in a field, which a man found and covered up; then in his joy he goes and sells all that he has and buys that field."[29]

The Kingdom is proffered as a gift, a gift which awaits our acceptance. How we are to receive this gift is clearly outlined in the gospels. On one occasion, the disciples rebuked parents for bringing their young to Jesus. It was customary to bring children to the scribes for their blessing on the eve of the Day of Atonement. Perhaps the disciples reacted in this way because they resented the parents treating Jesus as a mere scribe. As Jesus' response is one of anger, we can assume that His indignation suggests that an important principle is at stake.

"Let the little children come to me . . . for to such belongs the Kingdom of God. Truly I say to you, whoever does not receive the Kingdom of God like a child shall not enter it."[30]

The vast majority of us can thankfully look back to a time when we never had to plan for tomorrow or even worry how today would turn out. This is not because we consciously left these matters to our parents, but that such matters simply played no part in our thinking. And, just as we unhesitatingly trusted our parents in all matters, including those relating to life and death, so too must we trust God.

Jesus also talks of the Kingdom as being a secret. At one point in the gospels He tells His disciples:

"To you has been given the secret of the Kingdom of God."[31]

But the word "secret" is used, in this context, in an entirely different way to how it is commonly used today. It is not a secret in the sense that only a few are permitted to know its nature. While the Kingdom is already in existence, most of us fail to recognize it. This is partly because it is not something physical which can be seen and handled. Nor can it be summed up in a body of doctrine. The mystery, or secret, is to be found in Jesus' own existence, in what He taught and in the kind of character He invites us to become.

Conclusion

The Old Testament vision of the Kingdom being established on this earth through the direct intervention of God is realized and recorded in the New. But the Kingdom is not established in one fell swoop, or by force; rather, Jesus teaches us that the Kingdom is at hand. Later in His ministry he talks of His Coming as establishing a Kingdom in this world which, while growing from small beginnings, will one day meet with total success. This total success is bound up with Jesus' teaching on the third stage of the Kingdom's growth, when it will be finally and fully established.

There is nothing in the gospels to suggest, however, that the Kingdom is built by man's actions – for it is in some very significant way already in existence, even if not in its complete form, and will continue to be so, whatever man decrees. But to say that the Kingdom is not built by man does not mean that mankind has no part to play in the Kingdom. The reverse is true. The Kingdom – or God's reign – is extended as people, both as individuals and as groups, accept the invitation God offers to become a certain kind of character. We now turn to a description of that character.

3.

Turning the World Upside Down

To treat New Testament teaching as a check-list of what we should and should not do if we are to inherit the Kingdom is to misunderstand totally the teaching of Jesus. The law cannot save. Only God can do this. And, in place of the set rules which many Jews believed offered a guarantee of righteousness, we are invited to become a certain kind of character.

This character is presented in the gospels as possessing four main attributes. While totally opposed to a formalized, pseudo-righteousness, we are told to love our neighbour to the same degree that we love ourselves. Similarly, we are called to reject the commonly accepted signs of worldly success, and not to covet possessions or riches.

Against Pseudo-Righteousness

There is, throughout Jesus' teaching, an overwhelming abhorrence of a religion which attends only to externals. Time and time again, Jesus warns of how the religious and the upright remain outside the Kingdom by attending only to right practice and ignoring inward commitment. Indeed, this hostility towards the self-righteousness of the religious establishment led to a running battle between Jesus and the scribes and Pharisees.

Jesus' distaste for a religion which concerned itself with outward display is more than apparent in Mark's account of how the scribes and Pharisees reacted to the disciples' eating with unwashed hands. Why, they asked, did the disciples fail to follow the tradition of the elders? Jesus answered with a passage from Isaiah, which underlined the essential distinction between outward practice and inward belief.

"This people honour me with their lips
but their heart is far from me;
in vain do they worship me,
teaching as doctrine the precepts of men."[1]

Jesus continues by illustrating how formal practices develop, circumventing the spirit of the law, giving as an example the commandment to honour thy father and mother. One aspect of this honouring was, of course, financial aid. Some of the traditionalists argued that the aid which should have gone to their parents had been offered to God in the form of a Corban. In fact, however, this was no more than a legal fiction which allowed a person to retain property while denying financial assistance to one's parents. God's word had, as Jesus pointed out, been effectively nullified by man's "development" of this tradition.

"For Moses said, 'Honour your father and your mother'; and 'He who speaks evil of his father and mother, let him surely die'; but you say, 'If a man tells his father or his mother, What you would have gained from me is Corban' (that is, given to God) then you no longer permit him to do anything for his father or mother, thus making void the word of God through your tradition which you hand on. And many such things you do."[2]

Jesus then turns to the traditional teaching on cleanliness, understandable in itself, and particularly so in the context of the Middle Eastern climate. This tradition focused on the danger of uncleanliness entering into man. Jesus inverts the entire concept, thereby challenging its established importance.

"Do you not see that whatever goes into a man from outside cannot defile him, since it enters not his heart but his stomach, and so passes on? For, from within, out of the heart of man, come evil thoughts, fornication, theft, murder, adultery, coveting, wickedness, deceit, licentiousness, envy, slander, pride, foolishness. All these evil things come from within, and they defile a man."[3]

Jesus emphasizes the importance of a submission to the will of God, which goes beyond the mere observance of the law, when, in quick succession, He reviews a number of Old Testament commandments. On murder, Jesus emphasizes the anger which underlies the crime, pointing out that we must also be aware of the anger which we excite in others, and that we must strive for reconciliation. Such views, it must be remembered, were addressed to a Jewish audience appreciative of the sacred importance of worship. In order to emphasize the development of the law, Jesus places the task of reconciliation above this duty.

The approach to adultery is similar. It is not that adultery alone is forbidden, but also the lust which is its root cause. Those who think adulterous thoughts are equated with those who carry out the act. Jesus similarly develops, almost beyond recognition, the notion of not swearing false oaths. In a truly Christian life, such oaths would be irrelevant. The obvious integrity of the individual would remove the need for such a guarantee.

The law relating to revenge is similarly developed. The Old Testament teaches an eye for an eye and a tooth for a tooth.[4] The Pentateuch not only condones revenge, but details the degrees of punishment. In contrast, Jesus instructs us not to resist the wrong-doer.

"But I say to you, Do not resist one who is evil. But if anyone strikes you on the right cheek, turn to him the other also; and if anyone would sue you and take your coat, let him have your cloak as well; and if anyone forces you to go one mile, go with him two miles. Give to him who begs from you, and do not refuse him who would borrow from you."[5]

Passive acceptance and selflessness could hardly be more unambiguously expressed. We are constantly urged not to be misled into thinking that outward observance is all that is required. In a passage known as "The Woes", Jesus, lamenting the pharisaical exploitation of the tithe rights, which extended even to small herb crops, demonstrates how strict adherence to the finer points of law can often be at the expense of justice and the love of God. Jesus uses this contrast to condemn those who subjugate justice and charity to the externals of apparent holiness.

Whom to Love

Much of the Gospel is an appeal to reject a religion which has been perverted by so many formalized dispensations that it could, in effect, be practised without moral effort. In its place, Jesus proposes a religion which is concerned, not with externals, but with these very moral issues and which, within broad guidelines, details how we should respond. One such guideline is a duty to love our neighbour, a duty explained when the scribes and Pharisees question Jesus about His claim to be fulfilling the law of the prophets. To the Jews, the law was not only a summary of all wisdom, both human and divine, but a secure guide to righteousness, or what was thought of as the proper relationship with God. And, just as Jesus couldn't accept this view of the law as a terminal revelation of divine will, so the Pharisees and scribes would not allow Jesus' claim to be fulfilling the law to go unchallenged.

During one of these debates about the law, Jesus is asked which is the greatest commandment. The question itself would have been an obvious one to put to Jesus, bearing in mind the rabbinical understanding of the law. The Law of the Prophets contained 613 commandments, 248 of which were designated positive precepts, and the remaining 365 prohibitions. These commandments were themselves further classified into light and heavy injunctions, depending on the issue at stake.

Jesus' response to this question demonstrates how all-embracing our love must be, emphasizing that the first commandment is to love the Lord your God with all your heart and with all your mind and with all your strength. This response would have been greeted without any expression of surprise. What would have surprised His audience was His stipulation that one must love one's neighbour as oneself, and His insistence that from these two commandments derive all the Laws of the Prophets.[6]

It is important to emphasize that self-love is not forbidden. On the contrary, God accepts this as quite natural and indeed good. Our self-love should not, however, exceed our love of others. This love, of others and of ourselves, is part of our over-all love of God. This trinity of love between God, ourselves and others provides a yardstick with which to judge our individual and collective behaviour.

How embracing the love should be or, as it is traditionally put, "Who is my neighbour?" is clearly illustrated in the New Testament. The most familiar example is the parable of the Good Samaritan, which debates the nature of discipleship, a theme which is developed throughout the gospels, and which is told in direct response to the very question "Who is my neighbour?"[7]

It begins with a man journeying from Jerusalem to Jericho, who is set upon by robbers who leave him half-dead. His pitiful state is seen by a priest, who passes by on the other side, and by a lawyer, who does likewise. It is a passing Samaritan, whose people were long-standing enemies of the Jews, who, on seeing the state of the man, expressed his compassion by responding to the victim's immediate needs, binding up his wounds and taking him to a nearby inn, and who, moreover, attends to his long-term needs by paying the innkeeper to look after him until he has recovered. Once the parable has been told, Jesus quizzes His questioner.

"Which of these three, do you think, proved neighbour to the man who fell among robbers?"[8]

The questioner replies:

"The one who showed mercy on him."[9]

To this Jesus responds:

"Go and do likewise."[10]

As everyone present was fully aware that the Samaritans were the common enemy, no one could have been in any doubt that the love demanded by Jesus must be unlimited. The parable demonstrated moreover that the person who possesses the secret to eternal life is not necessarily the lawyer with his knowledge, or the priest with his status. The secret, in this case, was possessed by the Samaritan, whose profession is unspecified and clearly irrelevant, but whose love was spontaneous and all-embracing, and not provoked by any specific interpretation of the law.

Jesus returns on other occasions to the issue of how comprehensive our love must be. In Luke, for example, Jesus states:

> "If you love those who love you, what credit is it to you? For even sinners love those who love them. And if you do good to those who do good to you, what credit is that to you? For even sinners do the same. And if you lend to those from whom you hope to receive credit, what credit is that to you? Even sinners lend to sinners to receive as much again. But love your enemies, and do good and lend, expecting nothing in return and your reward will be great, and you will be the son of the most high; for he is kind to the ungrateful and selfish. Be merciful, even as your father is merciful."[11]

It is this love which, we are assured, will make us perfect (a word used only on several occasions by Jesus[12]) or whole. Is this yet another example of how impracticable Jesus' teaching is? Or is it a reminder of how few Christians are willing to live according to this ethic?

Rejecting Worldly Success

The gap between human performance and the character we are invited by the gospels to become is again discernible in the Beatitudes. The Beatitudes which, in Matthew, are part of the Sermon on the Mount, are prefaced by the phrase "when He sat down", which, to Jewish eyes, enhances the status of these sayings. It was customary for the rabbis to sit down in the synagogue before beginning any teaching. The introduction: "He opened His mouth" is a standard prologue to statements which contain no reservations. Moreover, Matthew's comment that Jesus "taught His disciples", suggests that the Beatitudes were not instructions given on only a single occasion, but rather that they were the substance of Jesus' regular teaching.

Each Beatitude begins with the word "Blessed", which would more accurately translate from Greek as "the bliss of God". What is therefore being offered to those who embrace or live by the teaching advocated in the Beatitudes, is nothing less than the bliss which belongs to God, in other words, a share in His eternal life. The word "bliss" or "blessedness" is therefore another expression for eternal life, and an eternal life which is not only other-worldly, with a promise of future happiness or blessedness, but is, as William Barclay describes the phrase, "congratulations on present bliss".[13] Those who embrace the Beatitudes are being offered entrance here and now to the Kingdom which has been established in this world and is in the process of being extended by the very act of attempting to enter it.

On one level the Beatitudes are a collection of paradoxes, with the first, "Blessed are the poor in spirit", holding out the prospect of only the poor having the opportunity to inherit that which is of lasting value. In Luke, it is expressed simply as "Blessed are the poor".[14] The absence of "in spirit" makes very little difference to the inner meaning. In the Old Testament, the term "poor" underwent a change of meaning. It was first viewed in the way we use it today, when implying a scarcity of financial resources. It was, however, also used in reference to someone who is unable to resist the pressures of the world, and who is oppressed by the stronger forces around him. It was, in addition, used to denote someone who, because of his relationship with God, ignores the humiliation inflicted upon him by the world, and who retains his own integrity, believing that such humiliation is preferable to anything the world can offer.

The Hebrew meaning of poverty is therefore the matching of one's own inadequacies, and the transitory nature of the world, with a dependence upon God. The greater one's dependence upon God, the greater one's own consequent independence from the world. The promised reward for this attainment is nothing less than the Kingdom of heaven.

The second Beatitude, "Blessed are they who mourn, for they shall be comforted", continues the apparent paradoxical theme with the promise that only those who are truly brokenhearted will gain eternal happiness.[15] The second Beatitude has, however, a more fundamental meaning than that ascribed to it by some commentators. It does not simply refer to the sorrow we experience when we feel a failure. Nor is Luke's interpretation comprehensive enough. When Luke reminds us that "blessed are you that weep now, for you shall laugh",[16] he is alluding, presumably, to the Christian belief that those who maintain their faith, in the face of persecution, will not go unrewarded. The meaning of this Beatitude is not limited to the ephemeral sorrows of this world: it embraces the ultimate sorrow, the realization that, through sin, we have distanced ourselves from God. For those who are sorrowful to this extent, there is a promise of comfort.

The third Beatitude, "Blessed are the meek, for they shall inherit the earth", is difficult to understand today, largely because the meaning of the word "meek" has changed.[17] The word originally had two meanings, one describing the relationship of man to man, and the other man's relationship to God. The term "meek", as used in its original context, does not exclude righteous anger, if exercised on behalf of others. Jesus was Himself susceptible to such outbursts of righteous indignation, not when the religious establishment set out to mock or trap Him, but rather, when they attempted to prevent Him from doing good.

In Hebrew, the word is applied to one who accepts that he works within God's domain and who accepts whatever God wills for him. In return, so the Psalmist tells us:

". . . the meek shall possess the land,
and delight themselves in abundant prosperity."[18]

The meek shall be guided in justice and God shall teach them His way, grant them grace, plead their cause, beautify them with salvation and they shall inherit the earth.

The Psalmist also promises that the meek shall inherit the earth. This promise would then have been interpreted as prophesying the advent of the Children of Israel into the Promised Land. Over time, as we detailed in Chapter One, this inheritance assumed an additional meaning, although, for many Jews, the original meaning continued to command a following. This inheritance comes to be viewed as the coming of the Messiah, whose arrival heralds the beginning of the Messianic Age. Jesus teaches us that this event means even more. By becoming man, God initiates the Kingdom here on earth, and it is entrance to this domain which shall be the reward of the meek.

The fourth Beatitude, "Blessed are they who hunger and thirst for righteousness, for they shall be satisfied", must have struck a common chord among many of those listening to Jesus.[19] The labourer's wage was meagre, and, for those fortunate enough to obtain it, usually done on a daily basis, as we know from the parable of the labourer and his hire.[20] Failure to find such work brought the labourer and his family close to starvation. By expressing the desire for righteousness in such an immediately recognizable and extreme way, Jesus was demonstrating the intensity with which we should desire righteousness. Little wonder therefore that William Barclay should consider this to be the most demanding of the Beatitudes.[21] It exposes all too clearly why we fail as Christians. We fail, quite simply, because we do not desire enough to succeed.

Paradoxically, however, this Beatitude is also one of the most supportive, in that we are, thankfully, not judged by the extent to which we have actually attained righteousness, but rather by the extent to which we desire it.

In the fifth Beatitude, "Blessed are the merciful, for they shall obtain mercy", we encounter the same linguistic problem as in the third, in that the word "mercy" has a number of meanings in the Old Testament.[22] It is sometimes used as we use it today. It also enjoyed a wider meaning, as an act of kindness, and it is in this sense that it is employed in the Beatitudes, where it represents the kindness of God, first of all to His Chosen People, and then to humanity as a whole. It is a kindness which is constant and immutable, even in the face of our human transgressions.

This mercy, or outgoing love, is one which God wishes us to demonstrate by our actions. It is therefore a mercy which demands a revolutionary change in attitude. The Jewish law laid down no mercy for the sinner or for the Gentile. They came to believe that God rejoiced in the death of a sinner. Jesus, however, taught that there was the greatest rejoicing in heaven over the repentance of such an individual.

The sixth Beatitude, "Blessed are the pure in heart, for they shall see God", is one of the most familiar, largely due to Keble's poem.[23] As we have seen, purity, particularly in the later stages of the Old Testament, was defined largely in terms of ritual observances. Actions were prescribed and, if fully carried out, the individual was declared pure. Conversely, failure to meet these requirements left the individual in a state of impurity.

These ritual observances were quite wide-ranging in their scope, stipulating, for example, which animals were considered clean and therefore suitable for human consumption, and which were unclean and therefore forbidden. As already noted, further rules applied to washing before meals. This view stands the traditional teaching on its head, placing the emphasis on inward belief as opposed to public observance of specific rituals. This is one of the main differences between the Jewish and Christian concepts of what constitutes a correct relationship with God. Simply observing the law is not enough.

The seventh of the Beatitudes, "Blessed are the peacemakers for they shall be called sons of God", once again involves a word with a plurality of meanings.[24] Shalom, the Hebrew word for peace, means total happiness and prosperity. It also implies living in harmony with those around you. Peace, as described in this broad fashion, clearly means much more than the absence of hostility. Shalom describes the state of human perfection, both with respect to an individual's feelings of happiness, fulfilment and contentment, and in his relationships with other human beings.

Peace, when defined in this way, enhances the importance of our actions, particularly when they affect others and their attempts to achieve perfection. One only has to begin to think about all those aspects of our own physical well-being to realize just how comprehensive are the demands of this particular Beatitude. In short, therefore, all individual and collective activity falls within its ambit.

By the end of the first century, the Beatitude, "Blessed are they who are persecuted for righteousness' sake, for theirs is the Kingdom of heaven",[25] was being tested through persecution. As William Barclay noted, the word for witness and for martyr had, in the usage of the early Church, become synonymous.[26] The challenge of the early Christian lay in what he believed and consequently in how he lived the faith. And it was this radically new lifestyle, which we read of in the contemporary sources, such as the Acts and Pliny the Younger, which was perceived as a challenge to the status quo.[27] Ironically, while the faith has given rise to persecution, that persecution has itself often resulted in the further spreading of the faith.

As well as offering specific guidance, three general precepts are discernible in the Beatitudes. The first is the clarification of the fact that Christian morality is not merely a matter of adhering to laws of conduct, but also involves the development of a certain type of character. Secondly, while the Sermon outlines much of the moral law of the Kingdom, it is not a law which pertains exclusively to the individual or individual actions. It also applies to society as a whole, but society as it should be, not society as it was, and indeed is today. This ideal society can, however, only be brought about through the grace of God, when such precepts are enacted by individuals or groups. Thirdly, the Sermon, as we have seen, is not a detailed legal or moral code designed to update the existing laws. Had it been, its meaning would have been ephemeral, like that of any law. Its meaning is, on the contrary, universal and unlimited by time. The Beatitudes, constituting as they do a series of apparent paradoxes, reject spurious righteousness. At various junctures, the gospel also sets out what our attitude should be to wealth and possessions, and it is to this theme that we now turn.

Rejection of Possessions

The danger of riches is one of the clearest messages of the New Testament, one of the most notable examples of this being the parable of the rich man and Lazarus. While the ultimate reward for Lazarus is eternal life, the rich man is forced to languish forever in hell, just as Lazarus used to languish outside the gates of the rich man's home. The rich man sinned through his passionate concern for wealth and his wilful indifference to the suffering of the poor and the oppressed.

In Matthew, Jesus puts forward, and in quick succession, three important sayings which highlight the radical nature of His attitude to wealth and possessions. At one point, we are warned that no lasting treasure can be stored up on earth, and that what a person thinks of as having lasting value, will determine where his intentions and interests lie.

"Do not lay up for yourselves treasures on earth, where moth and rust consume, and where thieves break in and steal, but lay up for yourselves treasure in heaven, where neither moth nor rust consumes and where thieves do not break in and steal. For where your treasure is, there will your heart be also."[28]

It is then explained that the disciples cannot have two masters, or what might more appropriately be called divided loyalty.

"No one can serve two masters; for either he will hate the one and love the other, or he will be devoted to the one and despise the other. You cannot serve God and mammon."[29]

The message is not to be concerned with the matters of this world. Hence we should avoid obsessive concentration on possessions. Such solicitude is not a Christian virtue and should not therefore be cultivated. What Jesus urges is a detachment from material things and a concentration on other matters.

"Therefore I tell you, do not be anxious about your life, what you shall eat or what you shall drink, nor about your body, what you shall put on. Is not life more than food, and the body more than clothing? Look at the birds of the air; they neither sow nor reap nor gather into barns, and yet your heavenly father feeds them. Are you not of more value than they? And which of you by being anxious can add one cubit to his span of life?"[30]

It is in the parable of the camel passing, or more accurately not passing, through the eye of the needle, that Jesus' teaching on wealth is truly clarified and demonstrably shown to be in marked contrast to the belief of many Jews, that wealth was a tangible sign of God's favour. The background to this parable is also relevant and therefore worth penning in. A young man approached Jesus and asked Him what is essentially a Jewish question.

"Teacher, what good deed must I do to have eternal life?"[31]

It is important to stress that the enquirer's concept of eternal life differed dramatically from the Christian concept with which we are familiar. Jesus' answer is, accordingly, a response entirely in keeping with the Jewish idea of eternal life. To gain eternal life or, in Jewish terminology, to enjoy a proper relationship with God, the young man must keep the commandments. This incident is an example of Jesus' way of teaching. He replied to the enquiry in such a way that the enquirer begins to question his own conduct.

The young man said to him, "All these I have observed; what do I still lack?"[32]

To this Jesus replied:

> "If you would be perfect, go, sell what you possess and give to the poor, and you will have treasure in heaven; and come follow me."[33]

We then learn that the young man "went away sorrowful; for he had great possessions".[34] Thus Jesus' offer was rejected. And yet the incident is of more universal and lasting importance than this. It is at this point, when Jesus advocates the selling of all one's possessions, that we can discern the difference between Christ's teaching and the traditional teaching of the Jews, in effect a significant difference between Judaism and Christianity. To be a disciple of Jesus, it is not sufficient merely to obey the laws. We must strive to be perfect. Thus, while Jesus' initial response to the young man's question was entirely unremarkable, in that it propounded the traditional Jewish teaching in response to an equally typical Jewish enquiry, Jesus' subsequent elucidation, in response to the young man's additional question, was entirely untypical, wholly unJewish. As such, its effect must have been remarkable.

The instructive force of this incident, and of the parable which follows, retains its power, and the implicit requirements remain so difficult to embrace that we attempt to modify them. One example of this attempt to dilute the teaching can be found in the New English Bible, where the word "perfect" has been replaced by the diluted phrase "go the whole way", which, apart from all question of literary style, ignores the fundamental importance of the word "perfect".[35] This importance is apparent on another occasion when the word is used. During the Sermon on the Mount, Jesus outlines what is required of His disciples, stating:

> "You must be perfect as your heavenly father is perfect."[36]

An even more significant effort at weakening the force of Jesus' teaching involves a reinterpretation of the parable of the camel and

51

the eye of the needle. During His teaching on wrath, Jesus explains to His disciples:

> "Truly I say to you, it will be hard for a rich man to enter the Kingdom of heaven. Again, I tell you, it is easier for a camel to pass through the eye of a needle than for a rich man to enter the Kingdom of God."[37]

One proffered, and clearly much more palatable, explanation, argues that what is really implied here is the difficulty of threading a camel's hair through an eye of a needle. As such a task is difficult, but hardly impossible, we can conclude that untold wealth is not an automatic bar to entering paradise.

An alternative explanation, which enjoys the apparent benefits of some academic research, maintains that the "eye of a needle" referred to by Jesus in the parable is, in fact, a cryptic reference to one of the smaller gates into the city of Jerusalem. And, while it may prove impossible for a fully laden camel to pass through such a gate, it would require little effort for someone to off-load enough to allow the camel to enter. Thus the moral of the parable, interpreted in this way, is that, while a super-abundance may be a barrier to entering the Kingdom, a reasonable sum, as yet unspecified, does not pose any insurmountable problem.

A third example of an attempt to reassure us that a concern with riches does not imperil our souls can be found in one of the older biblical commentaries, edited, surprisingly, by Charles Gore, one of the most prominent Christian Socialists until his death in 1928.[38] This commentary makes a distinction between gross and net disposable income.

> Still more important is it to observe that riches consist in the money and other resources which are really, and not merely theoretically at our disposal. In England, for example, professional incomes are largely mortgaged in advance by the expenses unavoidable if the positions to which they are attached are held. A stockbroker can live as he will and where he will; an

officer in the army cannot; a working man may have far more money which he can spend on his own pleasures than a physician. Now it is this overwhelming temptation to self-indulgence which our Lord declares in almost all cases to bring with it the refusal of his yoke, and so the loss of the Kingdom which he proclaims.[39]

Despite such attempts, there is no easy way whereby we can dilute Jesus' message. Indeed, in Luke, we find that the definition of riches is extended to include the use of power.[40] If further evidence is required to demonstrate that Jesus' message was harsh and unpalatable, we need only examine the response of the disciples. It was one of amazement, bordering on incredulity. For the Jews, riches were a sign of God's favour. If the rich couldn't enter the Kingdom of God, then it was more than reasonable for the disciples to pose the question: "Who then can be saved?"[41]

To these enquiries, Jesus responds: "With men this is impossible, but with God all things are possible."[42] Such an uncompromising statement allows no room for the sort of diluted interpretations favoured by some theologians who perversely defend riches, by arguing that, through the power of God, all things are possible.

At this point Jesus has come down clearly in favour of one of the two Old Testament attitudes to riches. While there is an over-all suspicion of wealth, there are two strains of thought. On the one hand riches are viewed as a blessing, and in the Old Testament there are many examples of rich men, and even of women, such as the rich woman householder in the last chapter of Proverbs, who do not conform to the wicked stereotype. At the same time, however, the prophets express a profound suspicion of the corrupting influence of wealth. We have already remarked upon the collection of rules, whose object was to protect the poor from the rapacity of the rich, rules such as the Sabbatical Year, and the Jubilee. However, as already noted, the existence of these laws does not prove that they were generally adhered to.

Conclusion

The Kingdom is undoubtedly one of the central themes of the New Testament. It has been argued here that Jesus, through the Incarnation, initiated the Kingdom in this world, a Kingdom which is still in the process of growth. It has also been proposed that, by seeking admission to the Kingdom, we extend it. Entrance is gained by becoming the kind of character who looks, not just to outward actions, but also to inward motives, and who is not concerned merely with resisting the temptations of evil, but with carrying out positive acts. It is achieved by becoming someone who is concerned, not only with personal piety but also with collective sanctity. To see Christians accepting and living the invitation which the rich young man refused, entirely reshapes the kind of question which ought to be asked about the involvement of the Church and individual Christians in politics. Accepting the involvement of Christianity in political action, we turn our attention, in the next chapter, to the difficulties which Christians then must face.

4.

The Church in Politics

There are a considerable number of difficulties which one encounters when moving from being a certain kind of character to undertaking effective political action. These problems are considered in the following three chapters, beginning with what I understand by political activity and then examining how the Church is involved in it. The Church is important to this aspect of the argument, for the Old Testament message is one of collective salvation. God struck a covenant with an entire nation. Christ extended this covenant to cover all nations, and established a Church which was entrusted with the task of evangelizing. The term "church" is however used in a number of ways, each of which merits consideration.

Political Activity

To many people, politics is defined as that peculiar activity undertaken by a special breed of persons, called politicians. A closer inspection reveals the limitations of such a definition. Robert Dahl, an American political scientist, has defined political activity as the process of who gets what, when and how.[1] MPs, who, for many, are synonymous with politicians, obviously play some part in deciding who gets what, how much and how often. Their role is, however, only one aspect of the political process. Those MPs and peers who form part of the government are clearly more important to this process. Similarly, some senior civil servants wield more power than backbench Members of Parliament, as do those lobbyists who have access to the Prime Minister or senior Cabinet members. Their influence is, however, usually more ephemeral than that enjoyed by the senior civil servants. The media too, often enjoy a short-term role, helping to pressurize a government into or out of taking a particular action, as well as, in certain cases, playing a long-term role by mobilizing public opinion on major issues, such as EEC membership.

What is true at a national level, is also true of local government. A comparable range of non-governmental organizations help decide who gets what, when and how. Employers' associations and trade unions are two examples. At the very least, they can determine who does, or does not, get a particular job. When political parties, either in or out of office, begin to draw up an election manifesto, a whole range of interested groups are either invited to participate, or try to gain admission to such proceedings.

This view is still too one-dimensional. Politics, so we are told, is an ongoing activity. Therefore, those organizations representing workers – who, like doctors, nurses and auxiliary workers in the Health Service, help to implement policies – play what often amounts to a day-to-day role in affecting the outcome of official decisions. Similarly, so do the government quangos, whose duties range from policing the law (e.g. the Commission for Racial Equality and the Equal Opportunities Commission) to carrying out a watchdog role (e.g. the National Consumers' Council). All of these must be included in our definition of political activity.

Political activity is such an all-embracing concept that it is difficult to define precisely. One of the best summaries of the different usages of the term is given by Michael Oakeshott. Generally regarded as the foremost contemporary Conservative philosopher, Oakeshott, in his celebrated inaugural lecture, said:

Politics I take to be the activity of attending to the general arrangement of a set of people whom chance or choice have brought together.[2]

As with all of Oakeshott's ideas, this definition is not only pleasing for its style, it is also valuable for the emphasis which it places on the near universality of politics. Oakeshott underlines the point that political activity is not a professional occupation for the vast majority of the population. He also reveals how politics is not conducted exclusively at a national or local government level. Political activity occurs within all those organizations which "chance or choice" have brought into existence.

Just as politics cannot be cornered off as an activity undertaken exclusively by politicians, so the standards governing an individual's political actions cannot be compartmentalized or pushed to the periphery of life, for political activity is part of the very stuff of ordinary existence. Indeed, it is through such every-day actions that individuals resolve and effect their moral values. People who think that their actions are carried out in a moral vacuum resemble those politicians who believe that they are totally unaffected by political ideas or ideologies.

> "Practical men who believe themselves to be exempt from any intellectual influences", observed Maynard Keynes, "are usually the slaves of some defunct economist. Mad men in authority, who hear voices in the air, are distilling their frenzy from some academic scribbler of a few years back."[3]

One immediate objection which might be raised to the view of politics as developed here, is that there remains very little human activity which falls beyond its scope. A committed feminist, for example, might rightly conclude that the family is an institution through which political action can take place, in terms of who gets what, when and how; who controls the money, and to whom falls the pleasure and the drudgery of looking after a home and raising a family.

There are, of course, certain dangers implicit in such a wide-ranging interpretation. Such a comprehensive view of political activity, if unchecked by other ideas and values, contains within it the seeds of totalitarianism. At this point, it is worth underlining the wisdom of the Church in holding doctrines which balance the extremism inherent in any view. Truth is rarely encapsulated in any single view. Doctrines have to be held in balance, weighed against each other, if a one-sided attitude is to be avoided. So, for example, at the end of the last century, an over-emphasis of the Incarnation, to an almost total exclusion of other teachings, such as the Atonement, led radical Christians to adopt a political stance which maintained the inexorability of progress. The advent of World War One was therefore an event as unforeseen as it was unimaginable to the exponents of this view.

Had the group's Incarnationalism been balanced by an equal appreciation of the Cross and Resurrection, man's fallen nature would have been considered and would, assuredly, have complicated the rather simplistic political analysis proposed by these Christian activists. Conservatives likewise distort the debate by conversely over-emphasizing man's sinful nature, to the exclusion of the promise of a Kingdom to be established and completed in this world. The near universality of politics needs, similarly, to be "balanced" with the importance which Christians attach to the individual, and the unique part which each of us plays in the Creation.

Accepting this wider definition of politics, in what ways can it be said that the Church is or is not, can or cannot be, involved in the political process? The difficulties in answering this question stem, in part, from the different ways in which the term "Church" is used.

One of the best summaries of the different usages of the term is given by Peter Hinchliff. In an article entitled "Can the Church 'do' politics?" he lists the four principal ways it is used:

* As a theological concept: the body of Christ.

* As the congregation of Christian people, either throughout the world or in its local manifestation.

* As a denomination with its institutional structure and organization.

* As the clergy or ecclesiastical hierarchy.[4]

At the end of the article, Hinchliff makes the strongest plea for Christians to become involved in politics. He concludes by saying that:

Christians cannot go into politics . . . They are there already and even political apathy will have political consequences.[5]

In contrast however, Hinchliff maintains:

"The Church" cannot go into politics in any way at all – except that it can and should make political *statements*, which will inevitably be chiefly negative and critical about moral ideals.[6]

While in complete agreement with his conclusions about the role of the individual Christian, I believe Hinchliff's conclusions about the role of the Church *per se* can only be supported if an unreal, limited, and indeed limiting view of political action is adopted. Hinchliff's explanation of the different usages of the word "Church" and of the possibilities of political action for each of these, merits analysis and discussion.

A Theological Concept

The first way in which Hinchliff uses the term "Church" is purely theological, meaning the body of Christ. Proceeding from this interpretation, Hinchliff presents two reasons why the Church cannot "do" politics. For Hinchliff, the Church can only be considered "holy" when viewed theologically. And, because it is holy, it:

Ought not to soil its hands by meddling in politics, which is a dirty game.[7]

Let us leave aside the assertion that politics is inevitably a dirty business – or any more dirty than any other business – and look more carefully at some of the assumptions underlying this claim. What is important, and it is a point made by Hinchliff, is that we live in a fallen world where our actions are inevitably imperfect. That being so, it would be utter folly to allow the Church in this sense (or,

I would argue, in any sense) to be allied too closely with political party programmes, or even politicians.

Being allied too closely or being identified with a political party or grouping of politicians does not, however, constitute the sole method of political action. Indeed, the major weakness of Hinchliff's analysis is his limited perception of what constitutes political action. To Hinchliff, politics is essentially about doing things, and excludes talking and debating about what needs to be done. By this definition, I, as a backbench Member of Parliament, could not be considered a politician. Practically all of my time is devoted to arguing for or against change. The scope for what Hinchliff would call "doing" is practically non-existent.

I speak in the House of Commons; I listen to my constituents and write letters on their behalf; with other local MPs I lobby both public and private bodies to help further the interests of the area. This lobbying is essentially verbal. Even when I see the Prime Minister about a local issue, I talk, while she listens. Admittedly, most of this talking is, hopefully, a prelude to political action. However, even my writing on fiscal and welfare changes hardly constitutes "doing".

Hinchliff uses the example of the Pope to illustrate the limitations of talking rather than doing. The papacy, he claims, is a relevant comparison because, as a result of the dogma of infallibility, the Pope has come to embody all four senses in which the term "Church" is used.

> He [i.e. the Pope] does so when he declares the truth in matters of faith and morals – when he *speaks*, in fact (i.e. ex cathedra), on certain subjects. But the cry: "Why doesn't the Church *do* something?" almost always intends "do" in sharp contrast to "speak". "Why doesn't the Church do something?" means "stop talking and take action". So that even a papal pronouncement that it was a mortal sin to vote for Adolf Hitler would not really count as the Church *doing* something.[8]

Here, Hinchliff has allowed this amorphous body of people, who seem to stand outside the argument and demand that the Church takes action, to determine how he logically considers the argument. One possible reason why he should espouse such a blinkered view of politics is that he, like the rest of us, has been conditioned by his own political background. Before becoming Chaplain of Balliol, Hinchliff taught in South Africa. He begins his article by recalling how his African students, at times of crisis, would pose the question: "Why doesn't the Church *do* something?" The emphasis on the word "do" may well be appropriate for a country which does not have a system of parliamentary democracy. But it is clearly less appropriate for this country, where political activity is conducted within a framework which emphasizes the importance of saying something as a prelude to any action being taken, or in some cases for preventing any action from taking place.

A second reason why the Church, viewed as a theological concept, cannot "do politics" is precisely because it is a theological concept. Who has ever heard of a theological concept getting its hands dirty? Who indeed? The misunderstanding again stems from the notion that politics "happens" only through people doing something. To view matters in this way is to emphasize the importance of achievement, while ignoring altogether the importance inherent in the very existence of an institution, or, indeed, individual. The importance of such existence is reflected in the Hebrew word for God, Yahweh, which means "I am who am".

Hinchliff's world of politics is, therefore, one without values, although those very values – or the physical culture – help to determine what is and what is not appreciated as legitimate political action. They are crucial, therefore, in determining the scope of traditional political activity. In no way, however, can political values "do" politics in the way Hinchliff envisages.

The Congregation of the Faithful

Hinchliff argues that the Church, defined in this instance as the congregation of Christian people, might conceivably take some kind of political action, at least at a local level. A local church might decide that its members should vote one way or another in a general election. But, Hinchliff adds: "It is not terribly likely that the members would do so".[9] Few would dispute this broad conclusion, although admittedly in some countries, such as Ireland, the faithful respond more positively to guidance on a limited range of issues, such as abortion and divorce. Hinchliff's contention is none the less interesting in two different respects.

First of all, the word "decide": by what precise means do people decide on political action? Second, there is a need to consider the range of political action it is reasonable to ask the Church, as a group of Christians, to undertake. Trying to get a congregation to jump politically one way or another, in a country with a two-, or what is now a three-party system, is likely to court disaster, purely and simply because to do so would be to misunderstand fundamentally what political action it is legitimate for the Church to take. However, a church may well take such a stand, even though many of the congregation reject the view put forward. To say otherwise would lead one to argue, for example, that the Confessing Church in Germany, in its exceptional circumstances, was wrong in its opposition to the Nazis, because it failed to carry all its members. What is considered legitimate or non-legitimate political action is an important question, and will be dealt with in greater detail in the last two chapters, when considering what constitutes a legitimate political approach for the Church as a local or national Christian community.

Before the discussion moves to the other two ways in which the term "Church" is used, it is important to pause and consider Hinchliff's comments on the difficulty of gaining agreement for political action by a Christian community. He reminds his readers that attendance at a parochial church council meeting shows "how unlikely it is that any decision should ever be taken by the whole of the local church".[10] The unspoken assumption here is that unanimity is an essential prerequisite for political action. This is clearly not the case, particularly in this country, where governments are invariably elected with less than fifty per cent of the vote, and where Gallup polls often show that, of the minority of voters who elect a government, a majority may be in disagreement with any particular political action followed by that government. Most political decisions are made after a great deal of discussion (or what Hinchliff dismisses as "speaking" rather than "doing"), and where the minority accepts the majority's right to make a decision against *its* (i.e. the minority's) interest. But such a process functions only if the minority accepts that the means by which the political decision has been made is itself legitimate and the topic under discussion is one which ought to be decided by traditional political means.

As a Denomination

The third usage of the term "Church" is as a denomination, and denominations have a machinery, whether it be a parochial church council, a local, national or international synod, for making decisions. Here, Hinchliff maintains, once again, that it is difficult for the Church to "do" politics as:

> . . . the function of these bodies is to legislate for or administer the denomination, or to speak on behalf of the denomination as a whole.[11]

To assume that these bodies are some kind of parliament is, according to Hinchliff, one reason, albeit a fallacious one, why Christians assert that the Church can "do" politics. Parliament has the power to legislate and:

> its legislation *will result in action*. There are coercive powers to be used.[12]

Two comments need to be made here, again relating to the limited view which Hinchliff has of politics. Is politics exclusively, or indeed primarily, about the ability to legislate and enforce decisions? If this is a correct view of the political process, then the role of the Opposition, and even many government backbenchers, is rendered redundant. Their role is merely one of talking, an activity which knits together practically everything else which goes on in Parliament. Talking is particularly important when trying to persuade the government that it is wrong. It is also important for government supporters who need to convince the electorate of the validity of their actions. Using the parliamentary platform enables parties, and even individuals, to take that debate out of Parliament, into the country and to the electorate. Indeed, given the strict whipping system of today's Parliament, where governments usually get their way, it is the debate which makes Parliament worthwhile.

Throughout each day, month and year, a continual election battle is waged to help shape the electorate's judgement.

Hinchliff's political world is also one devoid of pressure groups, or any of the other bodies which were reviewed at the beginning of this chapter. Pressure groups, of which the Church is itself a major example, help to shape political programmes, amend government legislation, as well as independently helping to determine the political agenda. To describe political activity in this country without mentioning pressure groups, is similar to a biologist attempting to explain the workings of the human body while omitting any reference to the blood supply.

While it is true that pressure groups can, and in some cases, do distort the political debate in favour of the more powerful and privileged, they are also an important means of communication between voters and their representatives, helping to give life to the political system in the same way that the blood supply carries oxygen to the brain. No political pressure group has legislative authority in the way Hinchliff defines it, although many of them can withdraw their co-operation and thereby make legislative action ineffective. And yet, pressure groups are a crucial part of the political process. The extent to which the Church acts as a pressure group within the British political system will be considered in the final chapters.

The Ecclesiastical Leadership

Finally, the word "Church" is used with reference to the ecclesiastical leadership, by which Hinchliff means the Church as a denominational institution, and the leadership of that institution. He does so in order to emphasize a crucial distinction which Temple made about the role of the Church and its members. "The Church", Temple maintained, must announce Christian principles, while Christian citizens have "the task of reshaping the existing order in closer conformity to the principles".[13] The role of the Church therefore, whether it is a synod, or the House of Bishops, as it would be in the Anglican Church, is to lay down general moral guidelines within which Christians attempt to "do" politics.

There is another political role for some Christians, one which Hinchliff concedes in the following way. Laymen, clergymen and bishops "will do all sorts of things that will be political things".[14] However, Hinchliff warns that it is "tremendously important" for those who occupy a position which allows them to speak out publicly and to be taken notice of, to say clearly whether they are acting with the moral authority of the Church or:

> . . . whether they are merely acting as Christian individuals, or groups of individuals, trying to do what they can within the limits of imperfectable human society. What is wrong, is to claim, or to even permit it to be thought that one is claiming, the authority of the true Church, the body and bride of Christ, in support of human and imperfect attempts at action.[15]

This distinction can be made clearly enough on paper, but how well can it be upheld in practice? Take, as an example, the Commission which the Archbishop of Canterbury established on the inner city and which published its report under the title *Faith in the City*. Had Robert Runcie not been Archbishop, he could not have established the committee which led to the report. Moreover, the response to the report shows how limited is the view which considers politics as only being able to take actions, pass laws and exert coercive powers to enforce decisions through established political institutions.

Faith in the City contains two sets of detailed recommendations, the majority of which are addressed to the Anglican Church in England. The second set of proposals suggests changes in government policy. None of these prescriptions has the force of law: even those addressed to the Church would have to be approved first by Synod and then, in some instances, gain the acquiescence of the Church Commissioners, who act independently of Synod. The impact of the report was none the less highly political, in the sense that action may be initiated to make major changes in how the Church uses its resources. The report also initiated a particular kind of public debate on the inner cities, the long-term consequences of which are, as yet, difficult to determine. In five years or so, the report may be recognized as having played a crucial part in changing the political debate, helping people to believe that there was an alternative to the way the Thatcher Government has performed since 1979. I believe the report will be seen to have played a valuable role, exercising considerable political influence, although its political effectiveness is in no way dependent upon the Church – when defined as a denomination able to marshal coercive action.

Is it right to use the term "Church" in the way it has been cited in the previous paragraph? The report was commissioned by the Archbishop of Canterbury, although the Synod did approve its establishment and funding. However, if the Archbishop had been acting in a purely personal capacity, would anybody have joined his Commission? More importantly, would the public have paid any attention to its results? Who would have taken seriously an invitation from Robert Runcie, announcing that he was acting purely in a private capacity, and not ex officio? What would the public have made of such a report drawn up by a Commission established by a private individual who was also – incidentally – Archbishop of Canterbury?

Conclusion

This chapter has argued that political activity covers much of our every-day life, and contended that only part of this is conducted by those people who are thought to be, by the narrowest of definitions, politicians. Furthermore, a great deal of politics consists of talking as well as doing. On this basis, the Church, both by its very existence as a sacred institution, and in the other ways in which the term is used, is unavoidably part of the political process. Here, however, its immediate effectiveness is constrained by the decline in religious adherence.

5.

Doubting Faith

The second obstacle in the way of operating an effective Christian attitude to politics is the marked decline in adherence to Christianity. We are not immediately concerned with the collapse of outward adherence, although this is important even if, as argued in the following section, somewhat exaggerated.

Much more important than this, however, is the collapse of a Christian vision of the world. This chapter looks at how Christian thought was challenged by the iconoclastic intellectual movement known as the Enlightenment, a movement which, by its rejection of tradition in areas of intellectual inquiry, was, on the whole, hostile to orthodox Christianity. It considers how that movement affected Christian thought, and reflects on how the Church should react to the floundering of that movement.

Starting From Belief

The Christian approach to understanding the world is not only very different to the non-Christian approach, but is, however regrettably, one which is currently pursued by only a small minority. As Christianity becomes a dying part of our culture, religious language takes on the aspect of a barrier to, rather than a conveyor of, meaning, and a loss of meaning results in a loss of effectiveness, whether one thinks in terms of evangelism or, more limitedly, of politics.

In 1939 T. S. Eliot gave a series of lectures which described the basis of a Christian Society.[1] He was essentially concerned with discovering ways of moving towards an ideal Christian state, and he wrote as if such a transition was both desirable and feasible. By 1943, his attitude had become much more pessimistic. In an address delivered in that year, Eliot broadened the debate, from language to feeling.

> The trouble with the modern age is not merely the inability to believe certain things about God and man which our forefathers believed, but the inability to *feel* towards God and man as they did. A belief in which you no longer believe is something which, to some extent, you can still understand; but when religious feeling disappears, the words in which men have been glad to express it become meaningless.[2]

Lesslie Newbigin, writing fifty years later, returned to the same theme in *The Other Side of 1984*, to which this chapter is heavily indebted. A comparison of Eliot's *The Idea of a Christian Society* with Newbigin's work illustrates just how radically the landscape has changed. Today, any detailed debate about how realistic it is to create a Christian society in this country, would be viewed as an exercise not dissimilar to that of counting the deckchairs on the sinking *Titanic*. Far from seeing a Christian society as an immediately realizable prospect, Newbigin's essay is written as though the Church is as small as it was in New Testament times, and his plea is for a strategy, commitment and missionary zeal, commensurate with that of the early believers.

The Enlightenment

The challenge, which has reduced Christianity to this minority status, stems directly from the Enlightenment, a blanket term used to encapsulate a whole process of intellectual change, beginning with the translation of Arabic writings into Latin; the impact of Aristotelian philosophy; a flood of misplaced and forgotten ideas which underlay the Renaissance, as well as the beginnings of modern science. The Enlightenment brought about a revolutionary change in man's perception of the world and, as Newbigin suggests, the name itself is significant.[3] It had been used to describe the decisive experience of the Buddha, and more importantly in

Christian terms, Jesus, who was the light come into the world.

The Enlightenment was not, however, a continuation of the Christian tradition, but rather a direct attack upon it. Instead of man being dependent upon God, man now sought to establish his independence from God, believing that what could not be reasoned, observed or experienced, was not truth. This was a direct challenge to the established Christian approach, as encapsulated in the words of Isaiah: "Unless you believe you will not understand."[4] To quote Newbigin again:

> Faith is not a terminus, but a starting point on which understanding can begin.[5]

In place of this approach, the Enlightenment substituted man-made reason, not just as a means, but as the sole means, of understanding and interpreting the world. The term "Enlightenment" highlighted, therefore, the fundamental change in man's perception of the world, from Faith to Doubt. In an age when man believed he was acquiring the knowledge to comprehend the universe independently of a God whose very existence was now questioned, nothing remained sacred or certain.

Of course this transition was not accomplished neatly or quickly. Pope's epitaph is indicative of just how long was the transition from Faith to Doubt.

> Nature and nature's law lay hid in night.
> God said *Let Newton be!* and all was light.[6]

Thus, even in the eighteenth century, the advancement of science could be seen as part of God's design. It was only later that science was to exclude God from any understanding of how the world worked.

The success of the Enlightenment in carrying all before it resulted in a shift in the position of Christian ideas. In contrast with mediaeval times, when a Christian view of the world embraced the life of the whole society, both public and private, religious influence was relegated to what Michael Polyani calls "specially privileged opportunities". Religious activity, in other words, was allowed on licence, providing its status was limited to that of any other private society operating within the state, and providing it accepted this reduced status.

Reaction

The Church's response to the Enlightenment is itself instructive, as Christians attempt to come to terms with living at the end of a period governed by its ideas. The initial response of the Roman Catholic Church was to put up barriers to the Enlightenment, through the operation of a twofold policy. One was to ignore the Enlightenment. When this became no longer possible, the Church reacted by attempting to stamp on its constituent elements.

The Protestant Church's response was different, but no less flawed. The Church gradually surrendered more and more of the debate to the rationalists. Instead of challenging the assumptions of the Enlightenment, it retreated into the pietism and the privatized religion which came to characterize so much of the Church's life in the early nineteenth century. In place of the mediaeval view of the Church's role, which embraced both the public and private domains of life, and the conception that human life can only be made sense of if considered in its totality, there arose the idea that Christianity was primarily a personal religion which, if it extended beyond the individual, was corporate only in that it covered the individual's immediate family.

It would, however, be foolish to accept uncritically the view of the nineteenth century as presented by the Tractarian propagandists.[7] A fundamental change was none the less occurring, with the dismissal of Faith as the starting point for understanding. There was moreover a double interaction at work. As this approach to thinking about the world gained credibility among churchmen, so did the Church, as a denomination, cease to attempt to teach the traditional view about the nature of knowledge. Such an abdication allowed the actual organization of the Church to become the purveyor of a doctrine which struck at the very roots of its own beliefs. This is an appropriate moment to warn of the dangers lying in wait for the Church if it too readily and uncritically espouses current intellectual fashions.[8]

It would be as wrong to think that the Enlightenment did not result in some enormously positive gains, as it would be foolish not to accept that, in general, the Church reacted in a negative and self-destructive fashion. This was not, however, a new struggle. As long ago as the eleventh century, Michael Psellos, a celebrated Orthodox philosopher-theologian, denied any clash between the process of reasoning and belief.

> "The process of reasoning, my friend, is neither contrary to the dogma of the Church nor alien to philosophy, but it is indeed the only instrument of truth and the only means of finding that which we seek."[9]

The Church is still struggling to determine the limits of Reason in our understanding of Faith. Michael Ramsey summed up this tension when writing of the criticism made by a group of Anglicans in the publication *Lux Mundi*.

> If criticism is allowed to modify thus far the presentation of faith, what if criticism questions the substance of faith as the creeds affirm it?[10]

Intellectual Counter-attack

What is clearer than ever, however, is that the dominance of the intellectual ideas of the Enlightenment is now subject to question. In particular, few people subscribe to the view that scientific advance invariably enhances the human condition. Indeed, many now view the gains made by science in the nuclear field as posing a distinct threat to man's very existence. Highlighting the opportunity which the Church now has to capitalize on the dwindling "faith" in the Enlightenment's approach, Michael Polyani is careful to pay tribute to the gains which have come about as a result of the Enlightenment, and his words need to be borne in mind if the Church's counter-attack is not to be seen as a mere negative, not to say reactionary, move. Polyani has noted that:

> The critical movement which seems to be nearing the end of its course today was perhaps the most fruitful effort ever sustained by the human mind. The past four to five centuries, which have gradually destroyed or overshadowed the whole mediaeval cosmos, have enriched us mentally and morally to an extent unrivalled by any period of similar duration. But its incandescence was fed on the combination of the Christian heritage in the oxygen of Greek rationalism, and when the fuel was exhausted, the critical framework itself burnt away.[11]

How should the Church respond to these changed circumstances? While it may be that it is not part of God's design that this whole process should be reversed, there is none the less a Christian obligation to try to discern what is planned for this world, and to co-operate in that design. To be part of that design, so the Prayer Book informs us, is to find perfect freedom. But, in "trusting the Spirit", and in our attempts to live according to God's design, it is all too easy for frail human beings to suggest that the Spirit commands us to do precisely what we anyway intend to do.

In his autobiography, Bishop Wand recalled an event, concerning a fellow bishop, which neatly illustrates this danger. The tale concerns:

> an elderly evangelical clergyman, who, having gone for the first time to a retreat, and, finding the silence intolerable, had decided to escape for the afternoon and find some conversation in the shops. Unfortunately he ran into the Bishop coming down the drive. "You see, my Lord," he stammered, "I am breaking my retreat but I have consulted the Holy Spirit and have been guided to do some shopping." "How odd", said the Bishop, "that you should both be wrong: this happens to be early closing day."[12]

How can we begin to think and plan the missionary task of the Church? The starting point is obviously to challenge openly the central assumption, or matter of faith, of the Enlightenment and, to begin arguing again (as, of course, some individual Christians have never ceased doing) that belief is the beginning of understanding. It is this assumption which constitutes what Polyani calls the "fiduciary issue."[13]

This entails putting Christian dogma, or Faith, back on to the agenda, in its rightful place, as the starting point. This is not, as Newbigin has emphasized, a plea to put the clock back and forcibly claim for the Church the dominant role it enjoyed in mediaeval society. Given the weakness of organized religion, such an approach could not be taken seriously. What is being urged is a promotion of a Christian perspective, or, in Polyani's terminology, a Christian fiduciary framework. From this basis, the Church can begin a dialogue with those in our society who live according to other beliefs.

According to Newbigin, the supremely critical dialogue which Christianity must now face:

> Is not a dialogue with other religions (important as that certainly is) but the dialogue with the culture which took its shape at the Enlightenment and with which the European churches have lived in an illegitimate syncretism ever since. Such a dialogue will always mean that our own basic presuppositions are called into question by the other party. Because of what I believe about Jesus Christ, I believe that this open encounter can only lead both the Church and the other partners in the dialogue into a fuller apprehension of the truth. This is not "dialogue insured against risk"; it is part of the ultimate commitment of faith – the commitment which always means risking everything.[14]

Conclusion

Modern culture is not shaped by Christian ideas, but is rather a product of the Enlightenment. While not for one moment denying the gains derived from the Enlightenment, this movement has brought about a revolutionary view relating to man's perception of his world. "Unless you believe you will not understand" has been replaced by a confidence in man's independent capacity to comprehend the world rationally. More recently, however, flaws in this form of rationalism have been perceived, thereby offering the Church a chance to move away from the "specially privileged opportunities" of its relegated position, to one of dialogue and effective political action. Central to this task, is the intention to put Christian Faith or dogma back on the agenda, and the following chapter considers how the recreation of a "clerisy", could act as the first steps towards this end.

6.

Renewing the "Clerisy"

The preceding chapter argues that religious knowledge is dying out. It is not altogether surprising that, in the aftermath of the Enlightenment, there should be such a significant drop in outward religious commitment. This does not, however, imply that one should concede the inevitability of total secularization, the consequence of which is the absolute negation of religion and religious values. The barriers in the way of effective Christian politics are explored in this chapter, through a critical examination of the use of the term "secularization".

This ideological warfare against the Church must be seen in its true context if, in the following section, we are to understand why, in addition to growing secularization, there has been a loss of confidence by the Church in conducting its missionary activities. How to move out from the specially privileged enclaves to which the Church has been relegated is then considered. Linked to this is the final theme of the chapter, which considers the place of folk religion in an outward-looking and confident Church.

Secularization

One reason for the loss of confidence shown by the modern Church has been the increasingly secularized nature of British society. While the debate is presented as mere observation of what is happening – i.e. fewer and fewer people are practising Christians – the term "secularization" has been described by David Martin as "less a scientific concept than a tool of counter-religious ideologies".[1] It is certainly employed in this way by students who confuse the decline in formal acts of religious commitment and worship with a decline in faith.

It is impossible to measure the current extent of religious faith, let alone embark on an exercise supposedly gauging it over any given period of time. Moreover, this apparent enthusiasm to explain away Christianity leads some critics to misrepresent the data on formal Christian commitment. An examination of the statistical evidence relating to secularization in England, is how Brian Wilson, in his volume, *Religion in a Secular Society,* illustrates both the danger of purporting to explain change in the extent of faith, as well as reading too much about formal religious commitment into the church attendance figures.[2]

Wilson examines the returns published by the Church of England, relating to the numbers and proportion of the population who are baptized, confirmed, attend Sunday School and who sign themselves onto the electoral roll. From these data he maintains that there are two discernible trends. The first is:

the diminution in religious participation over the period of some sixty or seventy years in most forms of religious involvement which amount to no more than one isolated ceremonial occasion.[3]

There is no disputing the trends indicated by the data, although the interesting aside about isolated ceremonial is not followed up. Why do people participate in such occasions? Wilson offers no satisfactory response. The other discernible trend is "the diminution in religious participation over the life-cycle of the individual".[4] As the individual ages, he is less likely to become involved in religious activity.

Wilson faces immediate difficulties over the baptismal returns. In 1962, the latest data available at the time he wrote, over half of all live births resulted in a child being presented for baptism in the Church of England. As regards this trend, Wilson observes:

We must allow that there is still a high demand for this ritual, but it cannot simply be said that this represents high religious belief,

77

especially in view of the evidence that this demand is not very extensively sustained by other religious practices.[5]

Wilson therefore resorts to explaining this discrepancy by referring to our "child-centred society", where:

baptism becomes another of those things which, in a sense, is every child's right.[6]

This view about a child-centred society may indeed be correct, although the growing figures on child abuse may cause some readers to pause. Even so, what are we to make of the phrase "every child's right"? No one thinks of rights when deciding for or against a programme of inoculation for a child. The advantages of such an action clearly outweigh the danger from any possible disadvantages. Why should Wilson contend that baptism should be viewed in an entirely different way, as an automatic action, as opposed to a spiritual act which confers admittedly less tangible, though undeniably equally beneficial, effects? Moreover, what place is there for religious rites in a supposedly secular society?

A similar comment is made about the numbers who are "'politically conscious' of their church obligation" and who place their names on their parish electoral roll. For:

although even on an electoral roll one cannot be entirely sure that all those names entered are deeply religiously committed people.[7]

What are we to make of the phrase "deeply religiously committed people"? Why should there be any interpretation placed on the electoral roll figures, other than the obvious one, namely that these people want to have their names recorded in this way?

The figures relating to the proportion of people marrying in church present similar obstacles to a straightforward secularization explanation of English society over the last hundred years. In the early 1960s, the marriage figures indicated around seventy per cent marrying in church. However, according to Wilson:

> set against other religious statistics, we cannot suppose that it reflects any change in sentiment concerning the religious nature of marriage as such.[8]

Why should these figures be set against others, and indeed against which figures should they be set? Hardly those set by Wilson. He construes reasons why each set of data cannot be accepted at face value. Once again, he is reluctant to allow these statistics to speak for themselves, to state, quite simply, the number of people who want to be married in the Church of England.

What then of burials from church, or under the form of a Church of England service, a final rite of passage? Wilson concedes that there is a widespread demand, but dismisses it in the following way:

> a man needs extraordinary presence of mind at death if he is to avoid religious officiation at his burial.[9]

This superficially helpful observation in fact misses the salient point that most people who do not believe in God do not reach this conclusion on their deathbeds, and few are likely to spend their last conscious moments arranging their own funerals. In short, those with atheistic views will have specified, long in advance, that there should be no religious funeral service.

There is clearly an alternative and equally valid interpretation of these figures, which suggests that the vast majority of people are at least uncertain enough about the existence of God to specify or allow a religious service at their funeral. Despite this, Wilson maintains:

> We can, however, except for the satisfaction of the mourners, discount this particular pattern of the individual's religious participation, which may or may not be voluntarily contracted.[10]

"The satisfaction of the mourners" is yet another of these throw-away phrases, so favoured by Wilson. Does their "satisfaction" support Wilson's own contentions, or does it in fact support the widespread religious adherence suggested by the figures?

For centuries, it is alleged, the Church of England has been seen as an ally of the powerful and the law-enforcing groups in our society. Local clergymen have taken their place on the Bench and, if they did not dispense justice more roughly than their lay colleagues, neither were they noted for being more lenient. For centuries, too, the English clergy was responsible for raising much of its own income from glebe lands, was also responsible for levying the Church rate and, if need be, enforcing payment. Throughout the last century, the Church experienced difficulties in gaining accept-ance in towns. The vast majority of churches operated a system of pew rents which, if it did not wholly exclude the poor, confined them, at best, to the free benches located in the least desirable parts of the building.

And yet, despite this record, over a third of all babies in the kingdom, including those whose parents adhered to other parts of the Church, are still being presented for baptism in the Church of England. The figures for confirmation are comparable. Despite the Church's failings, a considerable number of young children still come forward to be confirmed in the Church of England. The marriage figures are even more remarkable. The normal data released represent the number of people married in the Church of England as a proportion of those being married, whether for the second or the nth time. Once those marriages which cannot take place in church are excluded, it is apparent that the number of first marriages taking place in the Church of England remains around the fifty per cent mark, as it did in the 1950s, in itself a rate not far below the World War One level.

There are no equivalent statistics for the other denominations over such an extended period of time. What statistics we do have indicate that, between 1974 and 1982, the number of first marriages per thousand within the Roman Catholic, Methodist, Baptist and United Reformed Churches remained constant.

No matter how proponents of the secular argument present the figures relating to outward commitment, they continue to demonstrate a substantial body of Christian support, even if this is declining. How this base can be built upon is considered at the end of this chapter. However, this ideological warfare, waged under the almost clinically clean title of "the secularization debate", has had its effect – as was its aim – on the morale of the Christian community, as have other longstanding changes.

Loss of Confidence

The secularization war is the latest in a whole series of moves which have contributed, in this country, to the Church's loss of confidence. If the full challenge which faces the Church is to be justly appreciated, it is necessary to take a longer time span than most commentators have so far done, as the changes within Britain, during the past one hundred and fifty years, have been dramatic. The most significant change has been the move from a rural to an industrially-based society. Many of the changes in the Church of England's social functions derive from this transition from a village- to a town-based industrial economy. The parish is now no longer the administrative unit for central government, and clergymen – thank goodness – are no longer the law enforcement agents in their locality. Moreover, the Church's traditional role has been largely taken over by secular agencies of central or local government. The dispensation of charity is now a function of the Supplementary Benefits System and not of the local parish priest. Education, to which the Church committed a major part of its financial and human assets, has been taken over increasingly by the State. Never before in its history has the Church of England witnessed such a transformation of its role. Not surprisingly, these changing circumstances, which have resulted in what might be called the Church's loss of its "little empires", has set in train a long and protracted debate about its future.

Two forces in particular have helped to undermine the Church of England's self-confidence. While there is little evidence to support the view that the Church won substantial acceptance among working-class town-dwellers, the census and other nineteenth century data do suggest that there was a high number of middle-class adherents. It was often from this social group that the two main religious movements of the nineteenth century drew their support and, in respect of the Tractarians, its leaders as well. While Evangelicalism may have initially thrown up an aristocratic leadership, its rank and file members were largely drawn from the ranks of the middle and lower classes. So, too, with Tractarianism. A similar religious movement in the late twentieth century would not now be able to draw upon a practising middle-class base. Of equal importance is the fact that the lost middle-class activists have not been replaced by support from the working-class communities. Any. group with too many chiefs and not enough indians is likely to suffer from protracted periods of scepticism about its future.

It is against the background of the ideological warfare waged by the secularists, and the loss of confidence associated with the changed role of the Church in the day-to-day functioning of our society, that a programme of regeneration has to be planned. Counterbalancing these powerful negative factors are some, almost equally important, positive factors which favour the Church's position. The period of decline associated with the loss of its functions to the State is now almost at an end. Education is the exception and here, what can be best described as an armed truce, exists between the two sides. When considering a counter-offensive, the Church has considerable resources in terms of buildings, financial assets and manpower.

Church's Assets

Church buildings are important for a number of reasons and, while it is easy to emphasize the financial burden, they are nevertheless crucial in providing the physical base from which the Church's mission is carried out. While the number of church buildings is admittedly declining, very substantial numbers none the less remain. At the end of 1981, the Church of England had a total of a little over 16,800 churches. The Roman Catholic Church in England and Wales in 1985 had a total of 4,334. The Baptist Church in 1984 had 2,064 and the United Reformed Church, 1,882.[11]

This total illustrates how well-endowed the Church is, in terms of buildings, compared with almost any other voluntary organization in the country. Despite the fact that not all of these buildings are in the best location, or of the most convenient size, they do, overall, amount to a range of assets which it is difficult to price.

While the Church of England holds considerable assets at diocesan level, its main financial assets are held by the Church Commissioners, and these stood at £2 billion in 1982. This figure excludes the value of churches and the value of the land upon which they stand, the value of parsonage houses and works of art owned by the Church.

I have left until last the most valuable of all the Church's assets, its clergy, religious and full-time lay workers. The Church's manpower is very substantial indeed, despite the fact that most denominations still exclude women from the ranks of the clergy. The latest figures released by the Church of England show that, in 1981, there were 10,985 full-time clerics. The Roman Catholic Church, in 1985, had a total of 6,718 diocesan priests in religious orders etc., in England, and a further 1,119 in Scotland; the Baptist Church had 1,492 pastors in charge; the United Reformed Church had 1,848 ministers; and the Church of Scotland, in 1984, had 1,348 ministers.

Renewing the "Clerisy"

Can these substantial resources be used more effectively to support the Church in its missionary role? In answering this question, three issues need to be considered. These are: what is the most effective way to teach people about Christianity, accepting of course that Faith itself cannot be taught? How can the clergy's role in transmitting knowledge about the Christian faith be strengthened? And, finally, can the Church raise the necessary funds to finance a major programme of activities which the answers to the first two questions will entail?

These questions are answered with exclusive reference to the Anglican Church, not because the other denominations have no role to play, but, quite simply, because my membership and knowledge of the Anglican Church qualifies me to answer these questions in a way not only relevant to the Church of England, but, hopefully, in a manner likely to initiate a similar debate in the other parts of the universal Church.

Let us consider firstly the question of finance. The annual expenditure on pensions and stipends for 1985 amounted to £112·1 million, of which £45·5 million came from diocesan and other sources, the rest coming from the Church Commissioners. Is it possible to re-allocate the Church's financial assets, currently used for the payment of the clergy, passing this responsibility to the laity, who are, after all, the immediate beneficiaries of the clergy's priestly functions? It would of course be important to design a scheme whereby the laity had a national, rather than a parish-based, responsibility for this payment. The reform would otherwise result in the clergy becoming the prisoners of the local laity, adding yet a further twist to the sectarian tendencies within the Church.

Whatever the difficulties in devising such a scheme, I do not believe the task itself to be impossible. The average weekly donation needs to be increased by about fifty per cent, from £1·22 a week, in order that this target should be achieved. Such a sum is surely within the realms of possibility, particularly if the laity could be inspired by the Church actively attempting to fulfil its evangelizing role. Moreover, as this financial objective is progressively achieved, a greater percentage of the Church's central income from investment can be used to finance other activities. It is to these activities that I now propose to turn.

There is one reason, above all others, why the major emphasis should be placed on considering the clergy's role and functions. While the support of this group alone will not ensure the redirection of the Church towards its missionary role, without its active support and participation it is unlikely that such a change of direction could ever be brought about. Coleridge attached a similar importance to a somewhat more widely based group which he called the "clerisy", a term which included all those in the learned professions. Though the latter's adherence to Christian beliefs and values can no longer be assumed, Coleridge saw the function of this group in a way which is helpful to our discussion of the clergy: the "clerisy" has a duty to safeguard, develop and disseminate the spiritual heritage of the nation. How can each of these three functions of safeguarding, developing and disseminating the knowledge of the Christian faith be carried out more effectively today?

A prerequisite for success on each of these fronts is the raising of the spiritual and intellectual attainment of the clergy. How can these roles be properly strengthened? For a long period of time, the Church had benefited from the work of university-based theology departments. Not only have many of their teaching members added to the intellectual debate, they have also been responsible for giving a basic theological training to a considerable number of Church of England clergymen. Recent cuts in university budgets are beginning to affect the number of departments and student places. Some theology departments have been merged to form more general religious studies departments (thereby displaying the view that all religious knowledge is of equal value and possesses equal truth).

To counteract such measures, the Church needs to improve the academic standards of a selected number of its own theological colleges, which ought to be inter-denominational, allowing other Christians to benefit from the historic resources entrusted to the Church of England, when it was clearly the national Church. These more highly powered theological colleges should aim to fulfil three objectives. The first should be to raise the all-round qualification of the students, so that they feel better equipped to take up their role in society, along the same lines that Coleridge anticipated for his "clerisy". The second objective should be for some staff and research students to undertake research relevant to the Church and the development of its role. The third objective should be to help priests develop additional skills, so as to allow them to play a part in the other changes suggested here, particularly as regards educational reforms.

Among the many qualities required of a successful cleric is the ability to preach and to teach. It is staggering to learn how little emphasis is placed on the development of these skills during a cleric's training period. Regrettably, few young clerics can preach. While not the most essential of skills, preaching is none the less an important aspect of teaching. The development of teaching skills is sadly neglected by theological colleges. From their very inception they have, quite rightly, concentrated on developing spirituality. Owen Chadwick's *The Founding of Cuddesdon* shows how necessary this was in the early days of the College, and clearly demonstrates the importance of developing a daily pattern of prayer, anticipating the time when the ordinand will be working as a cleric, often on his own.[12]

No matter how central the spiritual life of the cleric is, other routines are necessary, if he or she is to have a successful ministry. Imagine, for a moment, waking up as a minister in charge of an inner-city parish in Birkenhead, Birmingham, or even Bath. There the cleric is, alone, facing street upon street, or high-rise after high-rise, all full of people to whom he has been appointed as a curer of souls. How does he go about this task?

The solution, increasingly resorted to by the Church of England, is to initiate team ministries. While these may be successful in some instances, it is worth recalling that few successful parishes are ever amalgamated into team ministries, which are almost invariably born out of failure and neglect. The Church attempts to hide this failure by what appears to be an endless debate, centring on the need to dismantle the parish system. The parish, so we are told, is a product of an outdated agrarian society, whose structure has played such a role in minimizing the Church's success in an urban environment.

This line of reasoning confuses the consequence of failure with its cause. The parish system remains crucial to the Church's mission and, instead of endlessly debating ways of dismantling it, more time should be devoted to initiating reforms designed to improve its efficiency. At this point, it is interesting to note how Roman Catholic views on this very issue are developing, away from a ministry of the faithful, to the parish as a whole, beyond the narrow confines of their own Church to the needs and issues which concern the entire parish. Canon Byrne, parish priest of St Laurence, the Roman Catholic Church in the centre of Birkenhead, contends that:

> most of the older Catholic parish priests (a large proportion of the whole number) are still following that [i.e. the old] pattern. They give a good service to our own people, but little to the wider community.[13]

Byrne contends that younger Catholic priests challenge the acceptability of this approach, in the light of Vatican Two.

> My theology is that . . . Jesus came to preach the Gospel to the poor, to give sight to the blind, to open prison doors and to set the captives free. One could add that "the charity of Christ urges us . . . teach ye all nations, baptizing them and teaching them to observe all the things I have commanded you"; which would certainly mean loving God with all our hearts and our neighbour as ourselves.[14]

According to Canon Byrne:

> All of this has been made possible since Vatican Two. The Church has broken down so many barriers that it is now easy for a priest within his own parish to fulfil his primary function to preach the Gospel to *all* by word or example.[15]

Educational Reforms

A number of Church-based educational reforms are central to an effective dialogue with Britain's post-Enlightenment culture. A much greater involvement in this area could provide a structure for the priest's and minister's working day and, in so doing, help fulfil that other role of the "clerisy", namely, the dissemination of the Faith.

The 1944 Education Act lays down that schools should begin each day with an assembly, and that, in secondary schools, one period a week should be set aside for religious instruction. That the law is flagrantly ignored is common knowledge, the defence being that there are simply not enough Religious Education teachers. One reform which the theological colleges should consider taking on board, is the development of the teaching skills of priests, so that many of them will be able to perform effectively in the class-room.

As everyone knows, it is difficult to begin teaching the principles of the Christian Faith if young people have not been brought up in a favourable Christian environment. The Church should, therefore, consider two further reforms. The first would be to set aside funds so that, over time, it would, together with other denominations, become responsible for the training of an ever-growing proportion of primary school teachers. Teaching the Christian faith would be part of what these training colleges would offer to their students.

At the same time, the Church should reverse the decline in the number of Church schools. Any change in the balance of Church schools should be undertaken sensitively, although sensitivity does not, in itself, preclude determined action. In the first place, the Church needs to ensure that none of its present schools, and this applies in the main to secondary schools, operates a selective policy which undermines the comprehensive principle. In addition, any expansion of the schools should initially be within the primary school sector. The aim should be to have a church primary school in every parish. Such teaching in primary schools, and offers to teach in all secondary schools, would not only introduce the pupils to the main ideas of the Christian faith, but would also teach them what to do in church, and how to make them feel at home there. It would have two further advantages. Church primary schools would prepare many of the children for confirmation, which would mean that, even if most of them became disillusioned during adolescence, they would find it easier to return later. This work in the primary school would create a working structure for the daily round of many an inner-city minister. Such a strategy would also ensure that, over time, the minister would become a familiar figure to an ever-increasing proportion of his parishioners. The link with the schools would also facilitate the forging of other links with parishioners, and specifically develop the role which folk religion plays in their lives. It is to this theme that I now propose to turn.

Folk Religion

In evangelizing the Church, we should begin to consider much more seriously what is called folk religion. In a recent book, the Archbishop of York looked sympathetically at:

> the unexpressed, inarticulate, but often deeply felt religion of ordinary folk who would not usually describe themselves as church-going Christians, but feel themselves to have some sort of Christian allegiance.[16]

How can the Church, as part of its mission, build upon these feelings?

The extension of church schools will provide links with pupils and their families, and these can be built upon at each of those points of contact between parishioners and their local church. A balance needs to be struck here between encouraging and meeting the needs of the parish at each of the major rites of passage, and encouraging parishioners to understand what is entailed by a Christian commitment. Let me give an example of how to adapt practices to the spiritual needs of some parishioners, and a further example of an opportunity to set out clearly what is meant by a Christian commitment.

While many families still turn to the Church when a death occurs, the Church has yet to begin responding adequately to the issue of grieving. The dramatic failure of the Church, in this respect, is evident in an article by Peter Brotherton, in his parish magazine.

A few years ago now I recall attending a meeting of the Oxford Council of Churches at which a minister from the United Reformed Church told us that he had recently preached at the annual service held at the local crematorium for relations and friends of those whose ashes were buried there. He then stunned the whole meeting, clergy and laity alike, from all the main churches in the city, by telling us that no fewer than ten thousand people had attended the service. It was certainly the biggest congregation in England that year.[17]

It would be surprising if the needs of the people of Oxford differed from those of people elsewhere in the country. Most people would find it confusing to attend a requiem on All Souls Day. It would, however, be possible for the Church to think of a special service, perhaps on the weekend following All Souls Day, inviting all those families who have had a bereavement during the previous year, to attend. Contacts could be made immediately after these services, thereby providing the basis for subsequent parochial visits.

This is just one example of the role which "folk services" could play in an outward-looking Church. The main events in the Christian year, such as Easter, Christmas, Epiphany and Lent, should be celebrated by special services for the whole parish. Harvest festivals and even Mothering Sunday are further examples of occasions when the Church could reach out and let it be known that the services are for the entire area covered by the parish, and not just for the elect.

The other example concerns church marriages, which offer an opportunity of explaining what a Christian commitment means. I am strongly opposed to the sectarian drift within the Anglican Church, but such a stance does not mean an uncritical attitude to all those church practices which ostensibly fulfil its national role. While I believe that those who wish to deny a universal right to baptism are wrong, I do accept that a much more serious argument for reconsidering the universal right which parishioners currently have to a church wedding can be advanced.

This right is already limited by a minister's obedience to his bishop, who normally forbids the remarriage in church of anyone who has been married before and whose partner is still living. But the Government's new Divorce Act makes a reconsideration of the Church's policy more, not less, important. The Act allows divorce after one year of marriage. Put another way, the Government is stating that marriage need last for less than the average duration of a hire-purchase agreement.

This Act throws down the gauntlet to the Church, at a time when it is considering proposals for the marriage of those who have been previously married. These proposals entail a large amount of pastoral work with the couple involved, and it has been suggested that this time might be better spent in preparing for first marriages. If, at the same time, the Church could be given the power, in certain circumstances, to refuse to marry anyone wishing to avail themselves of a Church of England service, its ministers would be able to spend more time arranging pre-marriage courses. A willingness to attend such a course, which might last about twelve weeks, would be a sign that the couple had begun to appreciate that a church wedding, with its vows to God, was something very different from one organized at a registry office. I do not regard these demands as sectarian, although I accept that some people may perceive them to be. It would, in reality, be an example of the Church's openness, balanced with the maintenance of some form of Christian integrity.

Conclusion

This section has critically reviewed the way the arguments about secularization have been used in an ideological battle waged against Christian ideas. This ideological warfare, together with falling membership, has led to a loss of confidence by the Churches in their evangelizing role. Ways of counteracting this failure of nerve, centring on a key role for a revised "clerisy", have been considered as one part of the political activity which the Church should undertake. The Church has, however, other opportunities to participate in more generally acknowledged political activities, and it is to these that we now turn.

7.

The Politics of the Kingdom
Part 1

This chapter collates the arguments so far developed. For Christians, political activity should be thought of, not as a novel idea, but within the tradition of the Kingdom, with its roots in the Old Testament. There are, however, no blueprints for such action. Politics has to be viewed, therefore, as an approach. This chapter considers, firstly, a number of limitations which groups of Christians currently place on political activity, limitations which distort the vision of the Kingdom. Then, taking the term "Church", the political approach advocated here is further developed by examining a number of recent examples of political activity.

The arguments, as presented so far, can be summarized thus: how the Church and the individual "does" politics should be seen as part of the long tradition, stretching back to the foundation of Israel and the covenant made with Abraham and his successors. Because of the length and variety of this tradition, it is tempting for Christians to select only those areas which suit their immediate needs or prejudices. Such distortions should be avoided, if for no other reason than that they cripple the comprehensiveness of what has so far been revealed. As far as is humanly possible, the tradition must be embraced in its entirety.

This tradition, throughout the Old and New Testaments, is concerned with establishing a society which works in accordance with God's will. To the Jews, the concept of an afterlife was unintelligible. The task of building Jerusalem here and now was seen as a collective endeavour, with salvation as an idea inextricably bound up with the fulfilment of the covenant, which encompassed the entire Jewish people. The concept of collective salvation receded during the conquest and consequent exile, a development necessary for the continued survival of the Jewish religion. It was at this time that the Chosen People learned the liberating effect of realizing that each of them had a direct and individual relationship with God. To this extent, religion became personal and, while personal religion was, for a time, dominant, the older tradition of collective salvation, associated as it was with enforcing justice, was never entirely lost.

Both traditions are present in the revelation of the gospels. Jesus states that the Kingdom is at hand, suggesting that, through His Coming, the task of establishing the Kingdom has begun, but has yet to be completed. At other points in the gospel narratives, He gives the clear impression that the Kingdom will be fully established at the end of time. All three stages are of this world, though it is unclear to what extent the Kingdom, in its final stage, is exclusively confined to this world. The Kingdom, though incomplete, is present, and we are invited to enter by becoming a certain type of character. Many of the required attributes have a collective as well as an individual effect. They thereby help to sanctify the community. Our individual and collective actions, therefore, help transform the here and now into a more comprehensive vision of the Kingdom.

Current Distractions

There are a number of political standpoints currently adopted by various Christians, which restrict that vision of the Kingdom, as revealed to us through Scripture. The polarization of the debate in Britain, the attempts to prescribe the means by which the Kingdom grows, as well as efforts to equate Christian politics with some kind of blueprint, all merit consideration. Let us, first of all, turn our attention to the Left/Right split of the political debate by some Christians in this country.

The two principal strains of biblical revelation, the collective approach, and the emphasis on individual piety, are both currently present in Britain. What is limiting, is the way exponents of one tradition deny the legitimacy of the other. Each has a valuable role to play in helping us to appreciate what being a Christian entails. It is as damaging for a Christian to maintain that salvation, or the Kingdom, is exclusively about collective action, as it is for other Christians to deny that collective action has any intrinsic worth.

This polarization of Christians has been masterfully analysed by Edward Norman, in his survey of the Anglican Church's ecclesiastical leadership over the past two hundred years. The Christian approach to political activity in Britain, according to Norman, is divided into that attitude which would:

> seek to regenerate men individually to render them fit to change society, and that which, on the contrary, would first change society by immediate political means in order to create the conditions necessary for educating men into regeneration.[1]

This divide, between the individual and collective approach, is one mirrored in this country's political debate. Parties of the Right emphasize the overriding importance of individual initiative and self-help, almost to the exclusion of any form of collective action. The Left is equally stubborn, defending the principle of collective action to such a degree that individual action is seen, not only as erroneous, but even treacherous.

In his *Commonplace Book*, R. H. Tawney attempted to diffuse this false dichotomy.

> It will be said: "Abolish economic privileges, and there will be enough wealth for all to live, and for all to lead a spiritual life" . . . Now economic privileges must be abolished, not, primarily, because they hinder the production of wealth, but because they produce wickedness. But, supposing unearned incomes, rents, et cetera are pooled, will not the world, with its present philosophy, do anything but gobble them up and look up with an impatient grunt for more?[2]

A second, and equally limiting, view of the Christian political perspective centres on the growth of the Kingdom. Again, the debate is polarized between those who assert that the Kingdom will be established in an apocalyptic fashion, and others who strenuously maintain that the Kingdom's growth is one of such orderly development that it can almost be measured.

Ken Leech, who, recently, has done more than possibly any other single person to maintain and develop the F. D. Maurice tradition in this country, presents the former view in its clearest and most attractive form. Never one to miss an opportunity to chide middle-class radicals, Leech asserts that the Kingdom's establishment is not achieved by gradual or evolutionary means. He maintains that:

> however dear that gradualist model is to Christian people, both liberal and conservative, it does not find its basis in the Gospel.[3]

For good measure, he adds:

> The parables, as a whole, emphasize suddenness and surprise rather than gradual growth.[4]

Leech is correct in pointing out the limitations of the Gradualist School of Christians, which dominated Anglican social thought, from the last two decades of the nineteenth century up until the outbreak of World War One in 1914. The view that man was increasingly virtuous, and that the Kingdom's establishment was thereby guaranteed, was impaled on the barbed wire in the no-man's-land of World War One. The Christian Socialist tradition of Maurice and his followers has yet to recover fully from that iconoclastic event.

Criticism of the Gradualist approach does not, however, imply totally underwriting Leech's view about the apocalyptic nature of the Kingdom. To support his view, Leech draws attention to those parables which emphasize the element of the unexpected. C. H. Dodd chooses the same tales as examples of Parables of Crisis: the faithful and unfaithful servants, the waiting servant, the thief in the night and the five wise and the five foolish virgins.

For Dodd, these stories form part of his assertion, that the

Kingdom is established in its final form, and that there is no addition or new move to be made before the end of history.

These parables, he asserts:

> were intended to enforce His appeal to men to recognize that the Kingdom of God was present in all its momentous consequences, and that by their conduct in the presence of this tremendous crisis they would judge themselves as faithful or unfaithful, wise or foolish.[5]

Dodd maintains that when the Second Coming did not materialize, these parables:

> were adapted by the Church to enforce its appeal to men to prepare for the second and final world-crisis which it believed to be approaching.[6]

The God presented by those who select only the Parables of Crisis is revolutionary, and disinterested in preserving anything of His creation. As Ronald Preston has remarked:

> To thank Him for "creation, preservation, and all the blessings of this life" is outmoded.[7]

Dodd's view is limiting in two respects. First of all, it appears to ignore the possibility of the gospels having both an immediate message to individuals, whose lifespan is as short and whose end is as certain as its exact timing is unpredictable, and a broader message to society as a whole, which will exist in time until the end of history. It is also limiting in a second way, in the same way as Leech's view, in that it fails to take account of the whole record. It ignores the significance of the Parables of Growth. Dodd, of course, discusses these, but, not with the Parables of Crisis.

It is clearly essential to embrace fully both traditions, which are far from mutually exclusive. Critics of the Gradualist School are right to call attention to the Parables of Crisis. However, these parables must not only be juxtaposed with the Parables of Growth. The total implication of the Parables of Crisis must also be embraced. These draw attention, not only to the unexpected, but also to judgement. In much of current Christian thought, this idea has almost totally disappeared.

A great deal of attention was earlier devoted to those very parables which emphasize growth and development, rather than violent change. Their message appears unmistakable and tells us, not only about God's power, but about how it is used in this world. So many of the stories concern human beings, carrying on day-to-day activities, almost impervious to the momentous work of God's will, which is enacted through us. The sowing parables have a constant theme: a modest initiation by man on the one hand, in contrast to God's bountiful harvest on the other.

A fuller vision, therefore, of the way the Kingdom grows is to see God in both ways, in sudden happenings, as well as in measured growth. Both approaches can be seen in traditional political activity, particularly if a world, as opposed to a purely British, perspective is adopted.

A third, and equally distorted, view of the Kingdom derives from the need to make Christianity conform to some kind of blueprint. This approach takes a number of forms. The easiest targets are those who, acting as direct descendants of scribes and Pharisees, present Christianity as a mere checklist of do's and don't's. This crude fundamental approach can, somewhat surprisingly, be detected among those who would like to be thought of as representing a more contemplative tradition. William Temple is an example of this trend. Writing on the Christian's duty in society, Temple recalls that each of us:

is required in his civic action (e.g. voting) to promote the best interests of his country, with a Christian interpretation of the word "best".[8]

Not surprisingly, Temple goes on to say:

the aim of any formulation of Christian social principles is to provide that Christian interpretation or at least the means of reaching it.[9]

Charles Gore similarly explained a feeling of disappointment, not to say despair, at the lack of Christianity's impact on society by, in part:

the vagueness of our own ideas, and consequent uncertainty as to our methods and our objects.[10]

The blueprints of Temple and Gore assume the guise of a plea for a clear statement of principle. This view has obvious attractions, resting as it does on the assumption that what is required is a little, or sometimes a great deal more, study before all is well. A more appropriate, but possibly more accurate view, at the time when Gore and Temple were writing, would have been that the Christian message was only too clearly understood, and that the failure to embrace it stemmed from the revolutionary change it requires of us, rather than a confusion about what the message was. There is a further major objection to this notion of a blueprint. It is, essentially, a contradiction of the way Jesus taught, which, as we have seen, was largely through the medium of parables, allowing each of us to draw our own conclusions.

These are the three most common distortions of the politics of the Kingdom. Christianity cannot be neatly compartmentalized and locked into either a private piety or collective works. The Kingdom encompasses all our actions, both as individuals and as a community. Likewise, while the Kingdom is proffered as a gift, its growth is not to be restricted by interpreting it as an exclusively evolutionary or apocalyptic vision. Similarly, God's work is not governed by any manmade blueprint. No matter how sophisticated the plan, revelation constantly teaches us that there are no manmade short cuts to the Kingdom.

The total record suggests that, above all, it demands a certain approach to life. This approach, and the difficulties involved in seeing it through politically, can best be described by taking the fourfold classification of the Church, as developed in Chapter Four.

The Body of Christ

How does the Church, as the Body of Christ, "do" politics? As we saw earlier, Hinchliff's assertion that it was impossible for the Church to be political is not the view taken here, for the Church, by its very existence, and by the way secular forces react to its existence, is acting politically. The Church is political in other ways too, as the Dean of Durham has been quick to suggest. Reflecting on the Church as a supernatural body, the Dean writes of it as having been called:

> by God to be an effective sign to the world of the presence and promise of His Kingdom. Its given task is to work and pray for the coming of God's Kingdom and to bear witness to its present power in the lives of its members.[11]

This "effective sign to the world" is given by the Church living the Gospel, and this living is given shape through the sacraments and prayer.

There are, however, two considerable difficulties in writing about the sacraments and prayer in this context. Personal religion now exerts such an influence on Christians, that the social implications of the sacraments are disregarded. Even those who stress the distorting impact which this personalized view of religion has had on the Church, allow an individualistic interpretation of the sacraments to go unchallenged. And yet the sacraments and prayer are the chief bond between God and the members of His Church. It is important to try to re-establish the links between a sacramental religion and a comprehensive vision of the Kingdom, both in terms of its individual and its social impact as revealed to us.

Baptism is an initiation ceremony, as is confirmation, which implies that membership has been granted to that individual, making him a member of the corporate body of the people of God.

The importance of this membership was brought home in a TV broadcast on the day of the enthronement of Michael Ramsey as the hundredth Archbishop of Canterbury. Not unsurprisingly, the new Archbishop was asked to select the most important day of his life. The interviewer, and no doubt many of those watching at home, expected Michael Ramsey to choose that very day. Instead, and without hesitation, he chose as the most important the day of his baptism. It was on this day, so Ramsey asserted, that he became a member of the Church, and thereby a potential inheritor of the Kingdom.

The Eucharist is presented as an offering, by the congregation, to God. It is seen as an active union between God and the congregation. It becomes a corporate act of thanksgiving, and is, equally, an act of atonement for the sins of the world. The social and political implications of seeing the sacrament in these terms have been described by William Temple.

> . . . we kneel side by side in virtue of our common discipleship. Differences of rank, wealth, learning, intelligence, nationality, race, all disappear; "We, being many, are one bread." We receive the food which has, by its consecration, become for us the Body of the Lord, that it may build us up into that Body, so that as different limbs, but one Body, we may be obedient to His will, and carry out His purpose.[12]

Even more difficulty is encountered when discussing prayer. We are told of its importance, and how we may or may not conduct our prayers, but little of the exercise itself. Even the Church Fathers have little to tell us by way of definition.

How can we pray the Kingdom? This is a question which Charles Elliott attempts to answer in his recent work *Praying the Kingdom*.[13] He does so believing that most people feel that, while much is wrong with the world, and in their own actions, they are trapped within a system from which it is impossible for them to break free. Elliott challenges this feeling of powerlessness (a word rather over-used by the Left) when commenting on the power of prayer.

If we see prayer as a means of releasing God's power into the world, of enabling Him to pour His transforming love into the critical centres of decision-making and activity, we begin to see paradoxically that we are not powerless at all. Our power to transform the world is God's power.[14]

The theme of the Kingdom in the Old Testament, and in the New, is presented by Elliott as mental exercise or prayer. Many of the main themes are presented as lessons which are still relevant to us today. In fact, He presents them as parables. Here is one example. The Old Testament message, promising an earthly Kingdom, is recalled. So, too, is the period when the Jews were subjected to slavery at the hands of the Egyptians. The record leaves little doubt about how oppressive the regime was, and how severe the punishments were for any attempted rebellion. It is in these circumstances that, through Moses, God promises the Israelites a release from their bondage.

Here, as today, is the test of the extent to which people are prepared to trust God's promises. Elliott invites his readers to become one of the slaves working in the brick pit, knowing how much more intolerable their working conditions will become if any failed attempt is made to defy their masters. Elliott reminds his readers that:

> the coming of the Kingdom is today what it was for the Israelites in Egypt – essentially a matter of trust and courage.[15]

The Ecclesiastical Hierarchy

The second way in which the term "Church" is used, is as a general term for the clergy and/or the ecclesiastical hierarchy. Reflecting on the evils of our society, Gore reminds that they:

> are not the inevitable results of any unalterable laws of nature, or any kind of inexorable necessity, but are the fruits of human blindness, wilfulness, avarice and selfishness on the widest scale

and in the long course of history; and that therefore their alteration demands something more than legislative and external changes, necessary as these may be: it demands a fundamental change of the spirit in which we think about and live our common life, and conduct our industry, and maintain our international relations.[16]

How is such a change likely to come about? Gore does not think it will, initially, be through any spontaneous conversion of mankind, but rather, as in the past, through groups of men (and, though Gore didn't say so, women), inspired by prophetic leaders who understand the sources of evil and:

> who have the courage of faith, which combine them together to act and suffer in the cause of human emancipation, until their vision and their faith come to prevail more or less completely in the general mind and will.[17]

It is because I share this view of how change may be brought about that I proposed a reformation of the "clerisy" in Chapter Four. It is the link between the leadership and the parochial clergy which is important here. While prophetic leadership is one of God's gifts, which may or may not be bestowed on current incumbents, a number of important practical steps, centring around a reformed "clerisy", can be taken. Indeed, for the hierarchy to will these changes may be one practical expression of prophetic leadership.

Crucial to any reformation of the "clerisy", is the role of theological colleges. A case was made out earlier for the Church of England to put more of its funds into the education and training of priests, that this would be best achieved by upgrading the status and resources of existing colleges, and that this move should be made if possible in conjunction with other churches so that the Church of England begins to share its historic resources with its sibling churches.

This reform of theological colleges was presented earlier as a means of raising the status, skills and spirituality of the clergy. It could also have a profound effect on the quality of staff. For these colleges to be viewed more as university theology departments, and for them to command more of the Church's resources, would result in a career structure which is at present lacking for the teaching staff. This must, to some extent, affect the quality of people prepared to undertake the work. The aim is for these colleges to become theological centres, to which the bishops and synod can turn for assistance and guidance, not only in areas such as the reform of the liturgy, but also within the wider social and political debate.

This proposal for a major theological input into the debate is, I fully realize, not a plea usually made on behalf of the Church. A more typical approach is to be found in Denys Munby's essay "The importance of technical competence", where he remarks that few Christian theologians or church leaders have any training in the social sciences.[18] Though, according to Munby, this is in itself not a matter of indifference:

> it is not a matter of indifference that, in Britain by contrast with America, there are only an insignificant number of posts in theological faculties dealing with "social ethics". It is not a matter of indifference that the authorities in the Church have no competent experts to advise when they venture to make pronouncement in these fields, and that they do not appear to be able to distinguish between an expert and a crank.[19]

Does the failure to make adequate use of social scientists constitute one of the major problems facing the Church today? What, anyway, makes an expert and who, but another expert, is in a position to choose one? The reality is that the Church is unlikely to regain its voice through better use of experts. What is required is to convey a vision about God's design and the nature of man. It is from this starting point that the Church ought to enter into the every-day political debate. During such a debate, experts from the physical and social sciences will, of course, have an important part to play. Their role will not, however, be one which determines the shape of the Church's contribution. Paul Ramsey, in a critique of the 1966 Geneva Conference on Church and Society, expressed the same view.

> In order for the Church to regain its voice and for the Church's Christians in council to speak for the Church in the world today, we must resist the temptation to believe that what needs to be done is to improve the Church's use of "experts". It is the aim of specificity in the Church's resolutions and proclamations that should be radically called into question. The better use of political or other experts to improve that might only make matters worse.[20]

A fuller explanation of what Paul Ramsey suggests is given in the case studies of political action with which this chapter concludes.

In the minds of many people, the term "Church" is synonymous with ecclesiastical leadership. Temple once remarked that, when people asked "Why doesn't the Church *do* something?", what they implied was that the Church ought to *say* something. This *saying* would, of course, be expected to come from a high-ranking member of the hierarchy. Temple certainly did his best not to disappoint anyone on this score.

One of his prodigious public announcements concerned the plight of the unemployed. This is worth recalling, because it illustrates that one doesn't have to be an expert to contribute effectively to political debate. The political response to Temple's statement is also illustrative of how the professional politicians then, as now, attempt to counter the Church's contribution when the hierarchy offers more than pleasant, inoffensive generalities.

Temple's plea was a call for the Government to increase the value of allowances to the unemployed, rather than make further tax cuts. In the 1930s, through the columns of *The Times*, he made "An Appeal To The Christian Conscience On the Subject Of Unemployment". Temple reminded his readers that:

It is not sufficiently recognized that national insurance was never intended to provide a subsistence level for the victims of an industrial slump, and the fact remains that, in many unemployed households, when the rent paid has been deducted from the total state assistance given, the margin left is frequently insufficient to provide adequate food for the family, let alone amenities such as may reasonably be regarded as necessary to the life of civilized people.[21]

Temple, therefore, made an appeal to his fellow Christians who pay income tax and:

who feel, as I do, that Christian regard for our neighbour requires us to seek first the good of those who are in greatest need to join me in letting the Government know our desire that, if the Chancellor of the Exchequer finds himself in a position to reduce taxation, the restoration of the cuts in the allowances for the unemployed shall have precedence over any other concessions, including remission of income tax.[22]

A few days later, the Chancellor, Neville Chamberlain, responded to Temple's initiative. He began by remarking that no Government, with any sense, would wish to see people idle, when they could be employed – a statement which is all too reminiscent of the current Government's attitude to the continuing unemployment problem. He went on to state that:

when people take a hand, whose influence, in consequence of their position, is likely to be widespread, then I think they ought to weigh their words carefully if they desire to rush into print.[23]

The Chancellor expressed the view that if the Archbishop had:

expressed his strong sense of the suffering and hardship which were being endured by members of the unemployed, and if [he] had stopped there, he would have had everybody with him.[24]

The Archbishop, however, did not stop there.

> He went on to express his views on the particular way in which
> the Budget surplus, if there should be one, should be employed
> in order to help the unemployed, and he concluded by inviting
> everybody who agreed with him to write to their respective
> Members of Parliament to say so.[25]

The Chancellor's response is revealing on a number of counts. He
attempted to deny the legitimacy of the Archbishop's move by
hinting that Temple had gone beyond his remit, while not stating
what he thought that remit was. He did not, moreover, dispute
Temple's contention that increasing unemployment allowances
would be the most effective way of raising the income of the
unemployed, apart, of course, from their obtaining work with
decent wages. He did, however, suggest that MPs should pay no
attention to any letters they might receive on the issue. He regretted
that anyone should suggest that:

> Members of Parliament are largely to be guided by the number of
> letters that they received urging one course or another, rather
> than by the exercise of their own judgement, being in possession
> of more information perhaps than others who are not members
> of the House.[26]

Setting aside Chamberlain's fatuous claim that MPs retain the
monopoly on all information relating to unemployment (the
unemployed, after all, know a little bit about the topic), the brutal
fact is that MPs actually are affected by the size of their post. More
significantly, in his subsequent budget, Chamberlain bowed to
pressure and redressed the cuts he had made to unemployment
allowances.

A more recent example of how political leaders are affected by
the size of their postbag, concerns the South African crisis. In the
summer of 1985, lobby journalists were given a background briefing
on the Prime Minister's stance. They were told why Mrs Thatcher

had felt safe to take up a position on South Africa which set her against the majority of voters at home, left her isolated among Commonwealth leaders, and hard pressed to gain any real understanding from her Western allies. She was firm in her conviction that she was right not to impose sanctions. She was, however, surprised by the silence of the churches on the issue. She had expected her postbag to overflow with requests from fellow Christians that she should support Bishop Tutu's call for non-violent opposition, which included sanctions. The Prime Minister noted, perhaps with satisfaction, certainly with relief, that no such flood of letters was forthcoming. The fact that she had received so few letters strengthened her resolve. Exactly how the Anglican hierarchy did react to South Africa is considered later, as a separate issue, and as a good example of how a Church should not "do" politics if it wishes to be taken seriously and, more importantly, to be effective.

The Congregation of Christian People

A third way the term "Church" has been used is as a general term of description for the congregation of Christian people, whether at a universal, national or local level. The first of two examples of political activity on this front concerns those Christians who constitute the Moral Majority. The second demonstrates how a group of committed individuals can function as a truly Christian community. Though very different in their aims and methods, both are examples of how the Church, in this sense, can "do" politics.

Many radical Christians assume that the involvement of Christians in politics would inevitably lead to a greater espousal of left-wing, or at least liberal views. The activities of the Moral Majority in the United States demonstrates the naïvety of such an assumption. It would clearly be impractical to attempt to offer a detailed analysis of the Moral Majority's views and activities – such a Herculean task would require an entire volume. What is of particular interest and relevance here is the Moral Majority's political astuteness in lobbying for the appointment of judges who are favourable to their views.

The Moral Majority's strategy is nothing if not amazingly simple: they locate and ruthlessly manipulate the pressure points. Supreme Court appointments are made by the President for life, and, given the balance between conservatives and liberals, a couple of additional appointees favourable to their cause would ensure that their views continue to be represented long after President Reagan's term of office expires. The Supreme Court fulfils the essential function of interpreting the Constitution. Appointment to this body can, therefore, exercise a decisive impact on major constitutional issues, as well as interpreting the legitimacy of current legislation, such as the legality, or otherwise, of abortion. The success of the Moral Majority's campaign can be measured by the appointment of Mr Justice William Rehnquist as the sixteenth Chief Justice of the Supreme Court. The President has been making similarly conservative appointments to other courts. According to a recent newspaper article:

President Reagan is set to appoint two-thirds of the federal bench by 1988, giving the conservative concept of "judicial restraint" momentum over the activist and liberal interventionism of recent decades.[27]

The Moral Majority has also been active in supporting organizations which screen judicial applicants for a whole range of appointments. One such body, the Center for Judicial Studies, is headed by James McClellan, a former aide to Senator Jesse Helmes, a Moral Majority supporter from North Carolina. The Center is said to have the co-operation and financial support of the Moral Majority Foundation and other right-wing groups interested in pushing their conservative agenda through the courts.[28]

The concerns of the Moral Majority are wide-ranging. In Anchorage, Alaska, fundamentalists have succeeded in reducing licensing hours. In Virginia Beach, Virginia, they stopped doctors from performing abortions. Elsewhere, they have pressurized textbook publishers, successfully persuading them to revise chapters on evolution to a pre-Darwinian view. Their influence extends to the banning of books from public libraries, and varying degrees of control of school curricula.[29]

This influence is not, however, confined to the United States of America alone. In New Zealand they have concentrated on proposals for reforming the laws relating to homosexuality. The key figure in the rise of this religio-political movement is Keith Hay, a building magnate and, for twenty-one years, Mayor of Mount Roskill. Under his guidance, the Majority has developed a two-pronged campaign.

It has organized a petition, canvassing and leafleting entire towns, using hordes of volunteers. The campaign has also paid for numerous mail shots and has strategically targeted certain marginal seats. The petition, so far signed by almost forty per cent of the adult population, has been constructed so as to reflect the number of petitioners per seat, together with the percentage of the electorate which supports the Moral Majority.

The campaign, under the guise of a Coalition of Concerned Christians, has also expressed its interest in issues as diverse as extending the censorship laws, a proposed bill of rights, a human rights commission, and religious education. Despite criticism of the Moral Majority's extremist views and methods, it must be admitted that these are areas in which Christians ought to take an interest. It is not, moreover, an adequate response for radical Christians to condemn the Moral Majority's abuse of the Christian message, as the Moral Majority can, and do, make similar comments about radical Christians. This is not a Left versus Right political issue.

There are, therefore, important lessons here for all Christians, the most important of which is that this real rift within the Christian community – for there are Christians on both sides of the debate – indicates the dangers of identifying the Church, as a denomination, with any particular political organization or party. Such an association makes the Church a divisive rather than a unifying force.

This argument, of course, relates to the Church in those countries usually referred to as Western democracies. Elsewhere the Church does, and should, play the role of a political party, as in Poland, where there is no democracy as we know it, or in the Philippines, where a democratic system is evolving, due in no small measure to the Church's intervention. And yet, even here, the Church's role is transitory. Political parties must eventually assume the role which, in a democratic society, is legitimately theirs.

The experience of the Moral Majority also underlines one of the main subsidiary themes of this book, the danger of depending exclusively on one part of the Christian tradition to provide guidance and increase our understanding. Much of their theology is based on a highly selective use of the Bible. The Bible is not perceived as an evolutionary record of a revelation which has continued beyond the time when selected books of the Bible were put together as a single volume. Entering the political fray, which we do all the time, is a hazardous task. It is even more difficult to do so as a Christian, particularly if that action is not accompanied by the humility which, tradition teaches us, is a prerequisite. Moreover, having condemned the Moral Majority, it is important to recall the parable of the mote and the beam, and to bear in mind the ways by which we promote our own political prejudices.

The second example is of how a local community of Christians can act politically or, as they would say, extend the Kingdom. The example quoted here is important in two respects. First of all, it demonstrates that Christian communities do not have to attend deaneries, diocesan or national synods, church councils, or wait for the leadership of individual members of the hierarchy, to begin giving effective witness to the Gospel. It also shows how local Christians can give witness to the fact that:

the God to whom the Scriptures bears witness is the living lord of history, not its absent architect.[30]

The story begins in the Wirral, with the closure of the Children's Hospital in Birkenhead. A group of Pentecostalists bought the building, out of their own funds, from the regional hospital board. Today, this church has a membership of more than seven hundred people. The Children's Hospital has been converted, indeed transformed, and now accommodates thirty-eight elderly people in a residential unit, and provides further accommodation for ten members of staff. The centre also runs a day nursery for forty children, each morning and afternoon, five days a week; a luncheon club for non-residents, with an average attendance of fifty people, also five days a week; a spina bifida unit for some twenty children; and a mother and toddlers group for mothers under pressure, which has a daily attendance of twenty to thirty every day of the week. There is also a sports complex in what was once the old hospital building, and the Christian Centre houses the Wirral Talking Newspaper for the Blind. Additional facilities include a recording studio, a graphics unit which had formerly been one of the Manpower Service Schemes, but which has now been turned into a small business, using the Enterprise Allowance Scheme.

This group of Pentecostalist Christians has now negotiated the acquisition of a second redundant hospital site in Leasowe, which is also in the Wirral, and which offers accommodation for thirty-five people in a long-term handicap unit, a hostel which will cater for thirty young people with various needs, including a drug rehabilitation unit. It is intended that the Leasowe site will include ten homeless family units, an unemployment resources centre providing a wide range of activities, including workshops in drama, music, arts, woodwork, pottery, and recreational activities. There are plans for a lecture theatre, with seating for a hundred and fifty people, and a twenty-four-track recording studio. The centre will also provide a market garden and play area for handicapped people. In the longer term, the Christian Centre intends to provide convalescent facilities and an extension of their residential homes, which will provide full nursing facilities. As with the Birkenhead site, there are plans for a luncheon club, which will accommodate fifty people a day, and a day nursery for fifty children, which will be open both morning and afternoon.

The aim is to increase the number of MSC jobs from eight hundred to around three thousand, as well as to add to the number of full-time permanent jobs. In serving the community, this Pentecostalist group has been as effective as any Christian group could be in today's circumstances. Most of the members are poor, and some of them are very poor. And, while government grants have been utilized, along with subsidies from both the DHSS and the Social Services, the initial capital outlay for the venture came from the pockets of the congregation. That first courageous step was an act of faith in a God whom the Pentecostalists see as the Determinant of history. If each local church council had the faith to match the witness of this particular group, then the writing of much of this book would have been superfluous. How the Church, as a denomination, can "do" politics, is examined in the following chapter.

8.

The Politics of the Kingdom
Part 2

The last way in which the term "Church" is used, is in relation to the church as a denomination, and it is in this sense that the Church is usually criticized as being political. Three examples of the Church's involvement in political activity are discussed. The report on the inner cities illustrates the folly of thinking that political influence can be exerted as though the Church still commanded the dominance which it enjoyed in the mid-nineteenth century.

Continuing church investments in South Africa draw attention to the limitations of the Church's call for political action, by the Government and other influential bodies, while, at the same time, being itself unprepared to embrace that very action.

The example of the Church of England's contribution to the nuclear weapons debate is one which, while it is unlikely to win majority support, is nevertheless a perfect example of what Christian politics, at a denominational level, should be about: an attempt to make the impossible possible.

1. INNER CITY POLITICS

The presentation of the Anglican Church's proposals for the inner city, published as *Faith in the City*, illustrates how inappropriate it is for Christians in general, and the Anglican Church in particular, to address the nation politically, as if the latter still constituted an active Christian body. The report is, none the less, an example of how the Holy Spirit can work through human inefficiency and error to achieve rather impressive results.

The Archbishop's Initiative

The official story of this report begins in July 1983, with the establishment of an Archbishop's Commission to:

> examine the strengths, insights, problems and needs of the Church's life and mission in Urban Priority Areas and, as a result, to reflect on the challenge which God may be making to the Church and Nation, and to make recommendation to the appropriate bodies.[1]

Two and a half years later, the report was finally published, and was accompanied by attempts by the Government to undermine its findings. One cabinet minister is said to have had his press staff working flat out to discredit *Faith in the City* as a Marxist document which should not be taken seriously. How the minister in question could be so convinced of the report's findings before its publication, remains a mystery. The hullabaloo which resulted from this interference not only ensured heightened media interest, in a report which might otherwise have gained a much lower profile, it also distracted attention from several criticisms to which the report was open, and which are relevant to the political debate under discussion here.

The first criticism is that the Commission did not address the correct questions. While the report is undoubtedly a first-class piece of work, it could have been produced by any group of well-intentioned individuals. What should have made it special, and distinct from purely secular analyses, was its theology of God's vision of the world, the nature of man, and his part in working out this design. However, instead of this being the starting point for the report, a theological perspective is merely tacked onto what is essentially a secular approach. The report, for example, begins, not with an appropriate scriptural reference, but with a reference to a Government white paper.

In this sense, the report highlights a major deficiency in how we preach the Christian message today. As already noted, the Christian Church, yielding to pressure from secular forces, has surrendered its prophetic role. No one should under-estimate the difficulties with which the Archbishop's Commission was faced. There is, however, a real dilemma here, for the Christian vision of the world is no longer in vogue, at least in this country. How, therefore, does one speak in a Christian language without sounding like a message in a foreign tongue? And yet, the Commission did not consider how this trend could be reversed.

The media hinted, at the time, that it was Norman Tebbit who had worked so hard behind the scenes to discredit the report. Appropriately, as it transpired, it was Norman Tebbit who was interviewed along with David Sheppard on Channel 4 News, on the day officially designated for the report's publication. During the interview, Tebbit illustrated how difficult it is for the Church to enter into a discussion with what is, ultimately, a largely non-practising Christian audience. At the start of the interview, Peter Sissons informed viewers that both Sheppard and Tebbit were committed Christians. Later in the debate, when Tebbit was asked whether he brought his Christian faith into economic affairs or whether he left it outside when he went into a Government department, he replied:

> Let me make it plain. I am not standing on Christian convictions about this because, apart from anything else, I believe now, and I think David acknowledges it in the book there [i.e. the report], that Christianity is a very minority group opinion, sadly, in the United Kingdom. So I speak just from a commonsense and humanitarian standpoint.[2]

Addressing a Non-Christian Audience

The second reason why the report was flawed concerns its advocacy of ways by which the Church can bring about change in a non-practising, though ostensibly Christian society. This weakness is clearly demonstrated by the gap in the report between diagnosis and recommended palliatives. The report does make a number of proposals by which the Church can, in the language of the New Testament, appear as "the City on the Hill". It also modestly suggests a small fund to finance inner-city projects. Beside the report's truly impressive analysis of the task facing the nation, such proposals are, however, revealed as wholly insignificant.

There are two decisive actions which the Anglican Church should have been asked to consider in the report. *Faith in the City* implicitly argued that one of the inherent weaknesses of British capitalism at the present time is that, in its thirst for short-term profits, the long-term needs of both society and the economy are sometimes forgotten. If this is indeed the case, the Church's argument would have been more challenging had it sought ways to use its £2 billion of assets to underwrite investment in inner-city areas, where returns will be below the current market rate.

The report appears to be similarly unaware of the role of symbols in our lives. As a symbol of the total change in emphasis, the Church could move its large bureaucracy from the plush environs of Westminster, to one of the inner-city areas discussed in the report. Apart from a small staff, necessarily attached to the Archbishop of Canterbury in London, the Church Commissioners, the Pensions Board and the Synod Office could all be translated. In so doing, the Church could more readily identify with, and pledge the regeneration of, one of the desperately depressed areas described in the report.

It was argued, in Chapter Three, that one of the central messages of the New Testament is the invitation to become a certain type of character. This invitation was accepted by the first Christians, who so lived out the message of the New Testament that they altered the society in which they lived. What the Church still fails to appreciate, is that the British electorate is usually more impressed by what people *do* than by what they *say*. This often constitutes a real handicap for politicians who find themselves on the Opposition benches. What the Archbishop's Commission failed to realize was that the Church, by putting into practice in its own affairs the recommendations of the report, would thereby have posed the most effective challenge yet to the Government's policies on the inner cities.

Separating the Poor

The third weakness of the report lies in the questions which it was asked to consider. While it is immediately newsworthy to address the problems of the inner city, particularly at the moment, an exclusive concentration on the inner city is not the most advantageous of standpoints. The Church of England claims to be the National Church. It cannot, however, justify this role if it decides to limit its brief in this way. A far better starting point would have been for the Commission to have been asked to address the problems of what the role of the National Church should be, and how this role can be made more effective. Inner cities and suburbs are inextricably linked, both geographically and conceptually, and one cannot rationally discuss one, while excluding its sibling. Had this been the Commission's terms of reference, the role of the National Church would have been clearer for all to grasp, and there would have been a greater appreciation of the Church's suggestions about the necessary re-allocation of the nation's wealth. No one on the Commission argued, as Tawney did, that:

> What thoughtful rich people call the problem of poverty, thoughtful poor people call, with equal justice, the problem of riches.[3]

Finally, the report details an enormous number of recommendations, for both Church and State, but says little or nothing about how this programme should be financed. Posing the right questions at the outset would have helped. The National Church has the task of presenting our duty towards our brother. As part of that responsibility is met through the fiscal system, it is particularly important to consider which measures to take to redistribute from rich to poor, from single and childless to those with children, and from the majority of the working population to those who are outside the labour market. No such detailed proposals were considered in the report. If the Church of England, and indeed any other denomination, wishes to be taken seriously in the traditional political debate, and to present detailed policy recommendations, which are, of course, not the sole way of contributing to the debate, it has to reinforce those recommendations with suggestions as to how they should be paid for and who should do the paying.

Surprising Results

While these are serious flaws, the unexpected result is that the report has exercised considerable influence on the political debate in this country. Part of Mrs Thatcher's political success has derived from widespread agreement that the 1960s and 1970s were an unmitigated disaster. By implication, therefore, the high public spending of that period, crucial to the maintenance of full employment, was similarly criticized. The first breach in this political dyke came with the debate which followed the publication of *Faith in the City*. When historians take a longer-term view of the Thatcher years, they may well find that it was the publication of this report, flawed as it is, which first prompted the electorate to consider that, even if there wasn't an obviously acceptable alternative to Thatcherism, one should at least be sought.

2. SOUTH AFRICAN POLITICS

The Anglican Church's stance on South Africa is a good example of how the Church should not "do" politics. The story is a long one, but the relevant lessons are to be seen through an examination of the policy of the General Synod and the Church Commissioners since 1982. It illustrates the irony of a body preaching to the Government while, at the same time, failing to implement, within its own sphere of influence, those very policies.

The Commissioners were established by Parliament in 1836.[4] They act as an independent corporation, although a majority of Commissioners are members of the General Synod of the Church of England. The Synod itself is the legislative body of the Church to which Parliament has delegated authority in particular matters. The Synod, as we shall see, passed a resolution in 1982, asking the Government and other bodies to disinvest from South Africa. The

Church Commissioners have themselves refused to implement this policy and, in so doing, have put forward a four-pronged defence. These four arguments constitute a good example of the Church opting for practical as opposed to ethical considerations. Even on practical grounds, however, the policy adopted by the Church Commissioners is open to question.

In 1982 the General Synod debated the question of South Africa, after which it passed the following resolution.

The Synod endorses the view expressed in the report *Faith in the Facts: The United Kingdom and South Africa* that progressive disengagement from the economy of South Africa and generous aid to the independent states bordering on South Africa, in order to promote their own economic and political development, is now the appropriate basic policy for this country to adopt as a contribution to bringing about peaceful change in South Africa, and asks the Board of Social Responsibility to enter into discussions with Her Majesty's Government and other appropriate bodies about how this policy might best be implemented.[5]

The belief of many members who participated in that debate was that the Church Commissioners, whose responsibility it is to manage the Anglican Church's substantial investment portfolio, currently valued in excess of £2 billion, were themselves members of a body with whom discussion about disinvestment would have to be undertaken. Four years later, and after the current wave of unrest in South African townships had begun, the Synod returned to the same question.

Prior to this debate, the office of the Church Commissioners issued "A factual memorandum" on South Africa, which put forward four main arguments as to why the Commissioners had ignored the July 1982 General Synod resolution, calling for progressive disengagement from the economy of South Africa.[6] These points each clearly merit consideration, as does a related report published by the Ethical Investments and Research Information Services (EIRIS), which examined the Commissioners' factual memorandum.[7]

Only Small Involvement

The Commissioners' first line of defence is that only a small part of their portfolio is invested in companies operating in South Africa. EIRIS has, however, produced two pieces of information which suggest that the Church's involvement in the South African economy is, in fact, considerably more significant than the Church Commissioners would have us believe. EIRIS' conclusion is based on the number of people working in South Africa for firms in which the Church Commissioners indirectly hold shares. Subsidiaries, or associates of British companies operating in South Africa, have a total work force of around 300,000 people. Those in which the Church Commissioners invest have a total work force of a little more than 117,000 people. Three-quarters of these people are employed by just twelve companies. Although one might dispute the practice of measuring involvement solely in terms of the particular size of a work force, EIRIS has concluded that:

> . . . it remains clear that the companies in which the Church Commissioners invest make up a very significant proportion of total British investment in the economy [i.e. of South Africa].[8]

The Commissioners were also shown to be investing in those companies with the largest involvement in the South African economy. There are forty-three companies on the Stock Exchange, each of which employs more than a thousand people in South Africa. The Church Commissioners invest in twenty-five of these. Of the twelve companies employing more than five thousand workers, the Commissioners invest in no less than seven.

The actual extent of the Commissioners' South African portfolio is also revealed by the proportion of their assets held in companies in South Africa. While twelve pence in every £1.00 invested through the British Stock Exchange goes to companies with more than five thousand employees in South Africa, 15–17 pence of each £1.00 of the Commissioners' investments is allocated to the same companies.[9] It seems, therefore, that since the 1982 synodal resolution there has been no discernible move away from investing in those companies with the largest operations in South Africa. Indeed, there is some evidence to suggest that the Commissioners are investing more money in such companies than the average investor on the London Stock Exchange.

Harming Beneficiaries

The second argument used by the Commissioners in their defence, is that to disinvest from such companies "would risk seriously damaging the long-term interests of our beneficiaries".[10] On this front, the Commissioners deploy a number of arguments. They report detailed holdings of more than £400 million (in 1985) of their UK portfolio which was invested through the Stock Exchange, and their statement of policy adds that about half of the present value of these investments is in companies with interests, of some sort, in South Africa. Since then, the Commission has downwardly revised this figure to £80 million.[11]

It is obviously more difficult for large investors, such as the Church Commissioners, to disinvest quickly from one particular area than it would be for a private investor to do so, or an organization with only tens of millions of pounds. The difficulties which they would encounter include the need to consider taking larger stakes in each of the other companies in which they already invest; gaining expertise and obtaining sources of advice on investing in smaller companies than at present; and re-thinking many of the conventional approaches to portfolio management in the light of the restricted portfolio open to them. EIRIS adds, however, that the majority of companies in the *Financial Times* all-share index, with a total value of £100 billion, do not have South African interests. A considerable choice, therefore, remains, even with a policy of total disinvestment.

The Commissioners argue, simultaneously, that they would not be able to maintain a balanced portfolio if they avoided South African-linked companies. It is noticeable that the Commissioners did not specify what they meant by a "balanced portfolio", against which it is possible to measure the effect of a particular ethical decision. To exclude companies with any South African interests at all, would mean ruling out completely some industrial sectors. However, the total value of all excluded sectors would be less than two per cent of the market as a whole. More importantly, it is possible to estimate the financial loss of operating with a more restricted investment portfolio.

While not everyone would accept the validity of those methods of measurement which are available, recent research, conducted by the City of London Polytechnic, on the basis of information supplied by EIRIS and data from the London Business School, helps to provide an answer. In a survey on the effect of placing a wide range of ethical restraints on investment, in areas such as alcohol, tobacco, gambling, armaments and South Africa, the City of London Polytechnic concluded that:

> . . . although company sizes were smaller and specific industry risks were greater in such restricted universes, the expected loss on a portfolio of £100 million, as a result of each of these criteria imposed, was remarkably small.[12]

Using a number of techniques employed in modern portfolio theory, the City of London Polytechnic concluded that, in none of the examples it studied, was the "cost", measured as a combination of capital and income, greater than £80,000.

Even if one takes the full £80,000 (or 0.08 per cent a year) as a rough guide, however, it will be apparent that this translates into only about three per cent loss over forty years. In comparison to the losses that might easily occur through bad advice or bad luck in a matter of months, this figure would appear rather insignificant.[13]

Enlightened Social Policies

The third part of the Commissioners' special pleading, is that they seek to ensure that those companies in which they indirectly invest, follow enlightened employment and social policies in South Africa. How does this assertion stand up to a closer examination?

If the performance of the companies in which investments have been made is compared with the EEC target minimum wage, then EIRIS found that, of the eleven companies in which the Commissioners invested considerable sums, ten were paying rates below the minimum working wage rate plus thirty per cent – the minimum target level for EEC companies operating in South Africa.[14] Moreover, as far as employment is concerned, a South African who is classified as black is three to four times less likely to obtain a job with one of the companies in which the Commissioners invest than a South African not classified as black.

A Legal Barrier

The final factor in the Church Commissioners' case for continued involvement in South Africa is that they cannot legally disinvest, as:

> financial considerations must be a major factor in all investment matters and this has been underlined by a recent ruling on the responsibilities of trustees and the management of charitable funds.[15]

In a letter to the Dean of St Paul's, who had enquired about the legal questions which have been raised, suggesting that the Commissioners would, in some way, be acting against the law if they disinvested still further in South Africa, Sir Douglas Lovelock, the First Estates Commissioner (i.e. the Commissioners' top civil servant) stated that the Megarry judgement on the miners' pension fund "is so starkly clear and so clearly relevant that one hardly needs a legal opinion on it".[16] The Megarry judgement followed legal action by the National Union of Mineworkers, who maintained that a larger part of the Miners' pension assets should be invested in industries operating in this country than is now the case.

The relevance of the Megarry judgement to the spread of the Commissioners' assets has been strongly challenged by Andrew Phillips, a specialist in charity law. Phillips draws a distinction between charitable and non-charitable trusts, which he believes is crucial to the whole argument.

The crux of the distinction between a charitable trust and a non-charitable trust is simple. The latter (to take as an example the case of the National Union of Mineworkers' Pension Fund, which was the subject of the Cowan-v-Scargill decision) relates to monies paid by individuals into a common pool *for their own benefit,* appointing trustees to administer that pool in accordance with the trust rules. A charitable trust, by contrast, is one where (typically) individuals provide funds not for their own benefit, but *for charitable purposes*. Indeed, so total is the difference from the private trust that it is a fundamental rule of charity law that a man cannot derive personal benefit from a charity he establishes.[17]

Ineffective Politics

In July 1986 Synod again debated the issue of South Africa, with the help of the memorandum prepared by the office of the Church Commissioners. At the end of its proceedings, it passed a resolution which, while calling for support for Desmond Tutu, urged "Her Majesty's Government . . . to deploy effective economic sanctions against South Africa", and continued by requesting:

banking and financial institutions, trans-national corporations, and all bodies with significant links in South Africa to take whatever steps in their power – including acts of disengagement – to increase the pressure on that economy, and urges the Church's financial bodies to give a clear lead in this direction.[18]

The resolutions passed by Synod in 1982 and 1986, and the reactions of the Commissioners to them, raise two important issues. The first needs only to be mentioned, and concerns the conclusion, evident from the above account, that the Commissioners are not directly accountable to the General Synod, in the sense that they do not feel constrained by the resolutions of that body. To whom they are actually responsible is an important and neglected issue, but one which falls beyond the scope of this present work.

The other issue concerns how the Church, understood here as the Synod and the Church Commissioners, believes it can bring about change. While listening to much of the July 1986 debate, I was struck by the impression of the extent to which the Synod believed the Government was waiting to learn of the Synod's view, before beginning to modify its policy on South Africa. Had the Synod followed the passing of the resolution by asking for a meeting with the Prime Minister – a request which was not even made! – I conjecture that the Prime Minister would have reacted in the following way. Her first question would probably have been to ask the Synod's representatives if they had yet implemented their own resolution and withdrawn their own assets. The delegation, no doubt, would then have explained the difficulties which they experience in Synod when attempting to persuade the Church Commissioners to comply. Before bringing the meeting to a rapid conclusion, the Prime Minister might well have suggested that she experiences similar difficulties with independent companies, when attempting to make such policies stick.

To ask the Government "to deploy effective economic sanctions against South Africa", as well as requesting corporate institutions to disengage financially, but not to do so oneself, is unlikely to be effective politically, or indeed to carry much moral weight. Acting as "the city on the hill" is an even more relevant political stance for the Church, in an age when most people are non-practising Christians. To the charge that it is mere symbolism, a sacramental Church should not be afraid to reply that it is, and that such symbols are a powerful way of demonstrating support for Desmond Tutu's non-violent opposition to apartheid. It would have had a profound effect upon the South African regime, which believes that the Established Church plays a more fundamental role in British society than it in fact does. It would, moreover, have increased the likelihood of a dialogue with the British Government, as a first step towards persuading it to alter its stance. Whether a policy of comprehensive sanctions by the British Government, as opposed to the Church, is proper, is quite another issue. Such a stance raises the question whether campaigners, Christian or otherwise, have the right to pursue a policy which may harm the innocent, in this case the majority of blacks in South Africa. This is not a new moral dilemma and is, in fact, central to the Just War theory, to which we now turn.

3. NUCLEAR POLITICS

The recent debate about nuclear politics is an example of how best the Church, as a denomination, a local group of Christians, or indeed as a federation of denominations, can effectively "do" politics. While I do not agree with the specific study recommendation of *The Church and the Bomb* – the Anglican Church's contribution to the debate – this study is none the less a notable example of beginning with a profound theological understanding, onto which is grafted the latest social and scientific knowledge, in an attempt to understand fully the issues involved.[19]

The General Synod of the Church of England, meeting in July 1979, considered a working party report on nuclear warfare and then agreed:

That this Synod, grateful that the Church's role in preserving and promoting peace has been opened up by this Report, urges the Board for Social Responsibility to explore how the theological debate relating to discipleship in this field might be more effectively and purposefully conducted through the Church of England in the light of the witness and insights of the whole ecumenical movement.[20]

The Board responded to the Synod's request by inviting people to serve on a working party which had the following terms of reference. These terms are significant for the way the Board believes that the subject should be approached. These were:

(i)   To study the implications for Christian discipleship of the acceptance by the major military powers of a role for thermo-nuclear weapons in their strategy.

(ii) To consider the bearing of this on the adequacy of past Christian teaching and ethical analysis regarding the conduct of war.

(iii) To advise the Board on ways in which members of the Churches can be helped to participate more effectively in public debate on these issues; and

(iv) From time to time to prepare for publication discussion papers on the matters under consideration.[21]

Church Involvement

The working party, which was chaired by the Bishop of Salisbury, published its findings under the title *The Church and the Bomb: nuclear weapons and Christian conscience*. The report caused an immediate and wide-ranging political debate, which, because it made people think about the ethics of nuclear warfare, was decried by many politicians who wouldn't have bothered, had the report fallen flat on its face. The familiar charge, issued by such individuals, that the Church should not become involved in political issues beyond general moral advice, was resolutely rejected in advance by the working party.

Whenever . . . Christian bodies engage themselves in detailed and controversial worldly issues, the cry is usually raised that they are not minding their own spiritual business and that they should return to that forthwith. This is unacceptable for . . . the dichotomy it implies between what is spiritual and what is worldly is a false one. Furthermore, it encourages the Church to play into the hands of governments, by allowing them to believe whatever they do will not be subject to critical scrutiny by Christians.[22]

The theological basis for *The Church and the Bomb*'s recommendations was outlined in a detailed discussion of the ethical considerations with which the Church has had to contend, when debating when Christians may or may not participate in warfare. This debate is usually known as the Just War Theory. This was followed by a section reviewing what the Old and New Testaments have to tell Christians about the quest for peace. The summary of the debate given here reverses the order.

One continual strand in Old Testament thought is of the creation being an act of God, the purpose of which is very largely beyond mankind's comprehension. Further, the Old Testament envisages the wealth of this world as having been given to all of us, on the basis of trusteeship. The use we make of this world's resources, therefore, offers us an active part in God's creation. This gift of freedom can, of course, be used either for good or evil.

The report also views the search for facts about the world and our attempts to understand them, as one of the other strands of Old Testament thought.

> Wisdom, in the sense of understanding and respecting the given order of creation, and of living in harmony with it, is goodness; folly, which means in essence ignoring that order and arrogantly flouting it, is sin.[23]

In explaining how mankind seeks this understanding, the report offers the best modern description of how a religious mind should work, in an age replete with the so-called social sciences.

> Moral thinking and action must be rooted in a profound humility before facts and a determination to live within the patterns and

limits of the created order, and not to do violence to them in order to twist them into some fantasy universe – which is the ultimate (and "original") sin of usurping the place of God. Christ also faces humankind with life lived according to the mind of God, an incarnation which takes the universe as well as humanity with the utmost seriousness. The findings (and warnings) of science at its best, the honest study of history and human sciences – these things are integral to a full and balanced Christian vocation, and provide both the theological basis for the kind of secular seeming exercise in which we are here engaged, and a firm hope that it will yield results that declare something of the will of God for today.[24]

Much of the report is a careful evaluation and summary of the technical knowledge then available on the subject of nuclear war. No authority on the subject has yet faulted the report on this aspect of its work, although some, of course, disagreed with the conclusions which the working party drew from this information. It was this combination of theological vision, combined with technical expertise, which so distinguished *The Church and the Bomb*.

It is from the Christian belief that God personalizes the idea of a moral being, that we gain an understanding of how His creation must reflect His moral order. Hence our search for it, and, even though we may grasp only a fraction of it, this exercise is the only one we know which, at least, has us heading in the right direction. Hence the importance of studying the universe, and our constant attempts to understand and evaluate what we find.

Church Tradition

At a number of points in the narrative, the New Testament presents Jesus as the link between God's design and human life, as originally foretold by the Old Testament prophets.[25] As we saw earlier, the essence of Jesus' teaching centres on our duty to love equally God, ourselves and our neighbour. This loving is the agent by which the Kingdom is extended. It is true that, part of the time, the gospels record Jesus' and His immediate followers' concern with what appears to be the immediate end of history. We see this particularly in the Parables of Crisis. However, at other times the dominating message is of the Kingdom's power being unleashed, and its growth in this world, as portrayed in the Parables of Growth.[26] It is this aspect of Jesus' teaching which conveys a message of concern about this world and all that goes on in it. As the Church began to grow, there is ample evidence of how the early Christians tried to apply the message of the Gospel to their daily lives.

> Contemporary ethical concern for secular issues, such as the one addressed in this report, is thus something which has roots in Christian tradition going back to New Testament times. A central conviction in that tradition has been the belief that this world is a place where the work of Christ can reveal its full meaning and exert its full power.[27]

It is from the time that Christians became active politically, in the established and restricted understanding of that term, that we have evidence that the Church sought to build up a body of teaching, as a basis for action. Part of their teaching wove the wider ethical tradition from Greek, Roman and Jewish practice and law into what generally became known as the Just War. Following the Edict of Constantine in 313, and, as a result of Christianity becoming a tolerated religion within the Roman Empire, Christians began to assume public positions within the State. Under Constantine, bishops were appointed judges, from whose court there could be no appeal. As a result of this integration of Church and State, it became part of the Church's teaching that it could be right, in certain circumstances, for Christians to wage war. Such a war must, however, be perceived as just, and Christians must fight with the right intentions.

The Church and the Bomb reminded readers of the full criteria which must be fulfilled in order for a war to be defined as just. The first concerns the resort to war, which must be undertaken and directed by the leaders of the State. The war must also be fought in a just cause. These criteria have become increasingly restrictive over time. The recourse to war must be a last resort. There must be a formal declaration of war and a reasonable hope of success. Moreover, the evil of the war must be outweighed by the expected benefits of victory. On all these counts the report questions whether a nuclear war can qualify as a Just War.

The conduct of the war itself must be bound by two further ethical considerations. The first concerns the immunity of non-combatants. The application of this principle has changed over time, as the nature of warfare has itself changed from limited engagements to one of total war, as in the fight against Hitler. Even then, when Britain was mobilized for such a war, the majority of the population was not directly involved in the war effort.[28] And what was true then is even more so now, in the nuclear age. Not unnaturally, therefore, the report recalls the moral impulse underlying this principle of non-combatant immunity: the desire to spare the innocent. "If war is necessary to protect human rights, it cannot justify attacking harmless people."[29] Given the acceptance that war may result in harm being inflicted on those not directly involved in the fighting, "this harm must not be deliberate and intended [and] such harm must itself not be disproportionate."[30]

The principle of proportion is the second ethical restraint on the conduct of war. Not surprisingly, the report questions whether a nuclear war can meet the requirement that any action must be an appropriate means of achieving the agent's lawful aims.

> In effect we have already argued that they (i.e. nuclear weapons) cannot because they cause civilian casualties. That apart, if the aim of the war is to restore justice, peace and order, then weapons which leave a wasteland behind them are inherently unsuitable.[31]

The report then considers whether nuclear weapons ought to be scrapped, or whether there is a valid case for retaining them, for the purposes of deterrence, concluding that the morality of even retaining such weapons is itself questionable.

Even if the West were bluffing, the general public would not know this; it is being asked to support policies which have the appearance of immorality, as also are the servicemen who have to be ready to carry them into effect.[32]

The report also questions whether a policy of deterrence, which has maintained the peace up until now, will necessarily continue to do so. Michael Ramsey has gone further by questioning the ethical basis of the argument that, because the consequences of nuclear weapons are so awful, no one will push the button, referring to this as a doctrine of "redemption of horror by horror". He adds moreover:

I suppose that it has a theological basis, though I find it hard to formulate.[33]

The Lambeth Conference of 1978 declared, as did previous conferences, that:

war as a method of settling international disputes is incompatible with the teaching and example of our Lord Jesus Christ.[34]

Important as this statement is, it offers no practical guidance to Christians as to how they should move from a general statement of principle to specific policy proposals. What *The Church and the Bomb* does is to provide an analysis which takes into account all the available information, places it in a theological context and then, in the words of the report itself:

. . . dares to make technical judgements and challenges the immunity afforded by more general statements.[35]

The report surrenders this immunity, while recognizing that any specific proposals, no matter how provisional, will, by their very nature, be imperfect.

Returning to the Issue

Recognition of this imperfection leads to another important aspect of successfully "doing" politics. Few political initiatives meet with immediate success, and *The Church and the Bomb* is no exception. One factor in successfully pursuing a political issue is a willingness to engage with opponents. In this sense, it is interesting to note the lessons which the Bishop of Salisbury, the Chairman of the working party which produced the report, has recently drawn from this political initiative by the Church. Similar lessons could usefully have been learned by the Labour Party, in its attempt to persuade the electorate of the feasibility of a unilateralist defence policy.

In a recent interview with Lord Longford, the Bishop admitted that he was by no means content with the way in which the working party presented its case. The Bishop accepted that there had been a failure to think through carefully how the report's proposals should be presented to the Allies. He also maintained that not enough care had been given to the timetable for phasing out this country's nuclear weapons. Nor had adequate attention been paid to the pressures which a UK unilateral declaration would have on our NATO partners. The Bishop did, however, envisage a practical role for the churches. He cited the need for them to set about actively breaking down the misunderstandings which underlie international conflicts. The Christian community, he maintained, could no longer be content with simply preaching the word.[36]

Effective Politics

Despite such omissions, *The Church and the Bomb* remains one of the best exercises of Christian politics undertaken by the Church (defined here as a denomination) in recent years. Its failure to win immediate acceptance is often the fate of radical proposals. Its strength and long-term importance lies in the fact that it takes the Bible as its starting point. The report then goes on to examine how the Church developed the concept of a Just War.

The fact that I do not happen to accept the policy recommendation of the report in no way detracts from the importance which I attach to it. There are practical reasons why, while accepting the main thrust of its arguments, I demur from its proposals. I do not believe that, at this stage, they are acceptable to the electorate. The public would, however, I contend, be more prepared to approve the cancellation of Trident, to demand dual control of American nuclear weapons based in this country, and to offer to negotiate Polaris. I am aware that some people would argue that it is difficult to balance this stance with the New Testament call to act as a city upon a hill. However, the practical concern of winning an election offers the chance of reducing the arms race and, indeed, of so much more besides. What can be said, with some measure of certainty, is that bridge-building, according to the precepts of the New Testament, is no easy task. *The Church and the Bomb* prophetically succeeds in maintaining the Church's tradition of realizing what, to man alone, appears impossible.

Conclusion

The Politics of Paradise argues that, as God has never forsaken the world, it would be utter folly for Christians to do so. The debate is not, therefore, about whether or not Christians should be involved in politics. We are, Christians and non-Christians alike, whether we recognize it or not. The debate ought to be about how our Christian beliefs should shape everything we do, including those actions which are political.

The concept of the Kingdom, the dominant *leitmotif* of both the Old and New Testaments, is crucial to the political process for all Christians.[1] It is against the backdrop of such revelation about the Kingdom that political activity takes place. Politics has been defined as who gets what, when and how. Each of us, as individuals, has the task of judging the extent of this. In doing so we should reflect the values of the Kingdom. As Christians, we also have a duty to make this a collective judgement.

One of the functions of the local church is to help relate this central message of the Bible to our lives. The task is not, however, simply a matter of "relating" in the normal usage of the term. Jesus is very clear about how we enter and, by entering, enlarge the Kingdom's domain. We are invited to seek it, and, while what we seek is a gift of inestimable value, it is one offered to each of us.

Political activity for the Christian is inextricably interwoven with seeking the Kingdom. Seeking the Kingdom is not, therefore, an intellectual game devised for our amusement. The quest is real and should dominate our actions as well as our thinking.

How do we know that our ideas are part of the true vision? Part of the answer lies with our conscience, which is one way whereby God speaks to us. Our consciences are activated by prayer, as well as by reading and communicating with fellow human beings. Our vision is also guided by what the Church has taught over time, as well as by what Synods, hierarchies and individual theologians currently contribute. Indeed, part of the task facing each denomination is to try to present a more comprehensive vision of what the Kingdom entails, thereby giving us direction. *The Politics of Paradise* has maintained that hasty political statements, often wholly secular in analysis and vision, are weaknesses common to all denominations.

What is required of the Church, as defined in this sense, is a more profound theological analysis, from which political conclusions should be drawn. The final chapter offered examples of this activity at its best. It is because this is such a strategic task that so much emphasis has been placed on building up this kind of expertise within the Church. If a traditional view of politics is adopted, this move would be unlikely to be worthy of comment, let alone be classified as political. Politics, it has been emphasized, should be accepted as a much more comprehensive activity than the traditionalists and secularists would have us believe.

A greater awareness of God's vision of the world, or, in other words, of theology, leads automatically to an extension of what currently constitutes the political agenda. The Gospel has been subject to such attack in this country that knowledge about Christianity is no longer part of common verbal currency. There could be no more important political objective, for any denomination, than seeking more effective ways of teaching the Faith. It is for this reason that a programme, designed to increase the Church's role in education, has been advanced.

In the past, many writers and teachers limited the universality of the Kingdom. *The Politics of Paradise* has considered each of these major restrictions because, when taken together rather than in isolation, they paradoxically offer a fuller appreciation of Christian politics. While it is wrong to think of the Kingdom exclusively in terms of the Church, as Ronald Knox has done, the Church has, nevertheless, a pivotal role to play.[2] Many of the proposals made here seek to increase its political effectiveness.

The evangelical view often conceives of the Kingdom as existing only in men's hearts. However, collective action cannot be divorced from the nature of the individuals who comprise such groups. The Kingdom cannot influence the group if the individual members ignore its message.

An evolutionary definition of the Kingdom creates different limitations. The argument has today swung so far against this approach that many British writers have now joined hands with the liberation theologists of the Third World. Their common cause is to stress those parts of the Gospel, and particularly the Parables of Crisis, which denote the imminent fulfilment of the Kingdom. They ignore, however, the fact that the gospels lay equal stress on the gradual growth of the Kingdom. The role of the political observer is to draw on those traditions, prevalent in a political culture, which most effectively contribute to an explanation of how politics is "done". Because of the nature of politics in Britain, the examples chosen to illustrate good political practice, ranging from the effective action of local Christians to the prophetic message of denominational leaders, has been along evolutionary lines.

The Kingdom cannot be encompassed within the programme of any political party. The weakness of the Christian Left in this country has been the judgement that:

Christianity is the theory of which Socialism is the practice.[3]

A moment's reflection confirms the absurdity of believing that a perfect God-given vision could be contained within the imperfect confines of a man-made ideology. The Divinity is, after all, incircumscribable. Any further reflection should be on the difficulties of defining what Socialism means.

A major reason for writing this book has been the long-overdue need to refute such an arrogant and distorted approach. The object has not, however, been to devise yet another blueprint. Moreover, as Jesus taught mainly through the medium of parables, the onus is clearly on each one of us to reflect on what He has taught, and for each of us to draw what we think are the relevant conclusions. Salvation is not to be found at the end of any shopping list. Only by exercising our free will, and fully trusting in God, can we truly seek the Kingdom.

Notes

Chapter One

1. Genesis 12:1–4, Genesis 17. At the time of the covenant Abraham was known as Abram.
2. Genesis 17:4–9.
3. 1 Kings 21:2.
4. 1 Kings 21:3.
5. 1 Kings 21:9–12.
6. Micah 2:1–3.
7. *Ibid* 3:2.
8. *Ibid* 3:9–12.
9. *Ibid* 3:12.
10. Isaiah 10:1–2.
11. *Ibid* 1:11–14.
12. *Ibid* 1:15–16.
13. *Ibid* 1:16–18.
14. Micah 6:8.
15. Isaiah 11:1–11.
16. Walter Rauschenbusch, *Christianity and the Social Crisis,* Hodder & Stoughton, New York, 1912, p.28.
17. *Ibid*, p.29.
18. Ezekiel 18:7–10.
19. Jeremiah 30:1–4.
20. *Ibid* 32:6–9.
21. *Ibid* 34:12–17.
22. Cited by Norman Perrin, *Rediscovering the Teaching of Jesus,* SCM, 1967, p.57.
23. The Rev. W. H. Bennett, *Social Ideals in the Old Testament*, National Council of Evangelical Free Churches, 1910, p.66.
24. Joshua 14:2–6.
25. Nehemiah 5:12–14.

Chapter Two

1. A. M. Hunter, *The Work And Words of Jesus,* SCM, 1973, p.90.
2. Matthew 3:2–3.
3. *Ibid* 4:17.
4. Mark 1:14–16.
5. Luke 10:9–10.
6. *Ibid* 4:5–9.

7. Mark 1:21–28.
8. Luke 4:31–37.
9. Matthew 4:23.
10. Luke 13:18–22.
11. Mark 4:31.
12. Luke 13:18–20.
13. Matthew 13:31 ("The Kingdom of heaven is like a grain of mustard seed . . .") and 13:33 ("the Kingdom of heaven is like leaven.")
14. Mark 4:31–33.
15. C. H. Dodd, *The Parables of the Kingdom*, Fount Paperbacks, 1961, p.36.
16. C. H. Dodd, *The Coming of Christ,* p.17.
17. C. F. D. Moule, introduction to Dodd, *Op. cit.*
18. Charles Gore, *Christ in Society,* George Allen & Unwin, 1928, pp.42–3.
19. Matthew 13:29.
20. Mark 13:26.
21. Luke 9:26.
22. Mark 13:32.
23. Luke 21:25–29.
24. *Ibid* 21:29–32.
25. *Ibid* 12:29–31.
26. *Ibid* 12:31–32.
27. *Ibid* 12:32–33.
28. Matthew 13:46.
29. *Ibid* 13:44.
30. Luke 18:16–18.
31. Mark 4:11.

Chapter Three

1. Mark 7:6–8.
2. *Ibid* 7:10–14.
3. *Ibid* 7:18–24.
4. Exodus 21:24. This law was, however, minatory. It is unlikely that it was applied literally and should rather be seen as a guarantee of satisfactory redress.
5. Matthew 5:39–43.
6. *Ibid* 22:35–40.
7. Luke 10:29.
8. *Ibid* 10:36.
9. *Ibid* 10:37.
10. *Ibid*.
11. *Ibid* 6:32–37.

12. Matthew 5:48, Luke 6:40. (The Revised Standard Version has, however, altered the translation, replacing "perfect" with "fully taught".)
13. William Barclay, *The Plain Man Looks At The Beatitudes*, Fount Paperbacks, 1963, p.11.
14. Luke 6:20.
15. Matthew 5:4.
16. Luke 6:21.
17. Matthew 5:5.
18. Psalms 37:11.
19. Matthew 5:6.
20. Luke 10:7.
21. William Barclay, *Op. cit.*, p.47.
22. Matthew 5:7.
23. Matthew 5:8. John Keble, "The Purification", in *The Christian Year*, Oxford edition, OUP, 1914, p.156.
24. Matthew 5:9.
25. *Ibid* 5:10.
26. William Barclay, *Op. cit.*
27. Acts of the Apostles, Pliny the Younger, *Letters*, Book X:9–10.
28. Matthew 6:19–22.
29. *Ibid* 6:24.
30. *Ibid* 6:25–28.
31. *Ibid* 19:16.
32. *Ibid* 19:20.
33. *Ibid* 19:21.
34. *Ibid* 19:22.
35. *Ibid* 19:21.
36. *Ibid* 5:48.
37. *Ibid* 19:23–25.
38. *A New Commentary on Holy Scripture*, ed. Charles Gore, Henry Leighton Goude, and Alfred Guillaume, SPCK, 1928.
39. *Ibid*.
40. Luke 16:11.
41. Matthew 19:25.
42. *Ibid* 19:26.

Chapter Four

1. Robert Dahl, *Who Governs?*, Yale, 1961
2. Michael Oakeshott, "Political Education" in *Rationalism in Politics and other essays*, Methuen, 1962, p.112.
3. John Maynard Keynes, *General Theory of Employment, Interest and Money*, Macmillan, 1934, Chapter 24.v.
4. Peter Hinchliff, "Can the Church 'Do' Politics?", *Theology*, September 1981, p.342.

5. *Ibid* p.347.
6. *Ibid*.
7. *Ibid* p.342.
8. *Ibid* p.343.
9. *Ibid* p.344.
10. *Ibid*.
11. *Ibid*.
12. *Ibid* p.345.
13. William Temple, quoted in Hinchliff, *Op. cit.*, p.346.
14. Peter Hinchliff, *Ibid,* p.347.
15. *Ibid*.

Chapter Five

1. T. S. Eliot, *The Idea of a Christian Society and Other Writings,* Faber and Faber, London, 1982.
2. T. S. Eliot, *Op. cit.*, cited in Introduction by David L. Edwards, p.39.
3. Lesslie Newbigin, *The Other Side Of 1984: Questions for the Churches.* The term "Enlightenment" is a translation of the German "Aufklärung".
4. Isaiah 7:9. This is a reference to the King James Version.
5. Newbigin, *Op. cit.*, p.24.
6. Alexander Pope, "Epitaphs: intended for Sir Isaac Newton." The counterblast to this epitaph came some time later, from Sir John Squire (1884–1958):

   It did not last: the Devil, howling "Ho!
   Let Einstein Be!" restored the status quo.

7. Any reform movement displays a marked tendency to exaggerate the particular problem or problems with which it is concerned. The Tractarians were no exception to this general rule.
8. E. R. Norman, *Church And Society in England: 1770–1970,* Clarendon Press, Oxford, 1976.
9. Michael Psellos, letter to Patriarch John Xiphilinos, ed. C. Sathas, *Miscellanea Byzantina,* Vol.V., Venice, 1877, p.447.
10. Michael Ramsey, *From Gore to Temple,* Longmans, 1960, p.14.
11. Michael Polyani, *Personal Knowledge,* 1958, p.265, quoted in Newbigin, *Op. cit.*, p.21.
12. William Wand, *Changeful Page,* Hodder & Stoughton, 1965, p.191.
13. Michael Polyani, *Op. cit.*, re Newbigin, p.29.
14. Newbigin, *Op. cit.*, p.31.

Chapter Six

1. David Martin, "Towards Eliminating Concepts of Secularization", *The Religious and the Secular,* Routledge and Kegan Paul, 1969.

2. Brian Wilson, *Religion in a Secular Society,* C. A. Watts, 1966.
3. *Ibid*, p.10.
4. *Ibid*.
5. *Ibid*.
6. *Ibid*.
7. *Ibid*, p.13
8. *Ibid*, p.15.
9. *Ibid*, p.17.
10. *Ibid*, pp.17–18.
11. There are no comparable figures available for the number of Catholic churches in Scotland.
12. Owen Chadwick, *The Founding of Cuddesdon,* Oxford, 1954.
13. Canon Byrne, "New Patterns of Urban Ministry". *Annual Review,* 1983, St George's House, Windsor.
14. *Ibid*.
15. *Ibid*.
16. John Habgood *Church and Nation in a Secular Age,* Darton, Longman & Todd, 1983, p.78.
17. Peter Brotherton, *Portsea Parish News,* November, 1983.

Chapter Seven

1. E. R. Norman, *Church And Society In England, 1770–1970,* Clarendon Press, Oxford, 1976, p.14.
2. R. H. Tawney, *The Commonplace Book,* Cambridge University Press, 1972, p.61.
3. Leech, Ken, The Kingdom of God: "The Regulative Principle of Theology", an unpublished lecture, 1981.
4. *Ibid*.
5. C. H. Dodd, *The Parables of the Kingdom,* p.130.
6. *Ibid*.
7. Ronald H. Preston, *Middle Axioms in Christian Social Ethics,* reproduced in *Explorations in Theology,* 9, SCM, 1981.
8. William Temple, *Christianity and the Social Order,* pp.27–8.
9. William Temple, *Op. cit.,* p.30.
10. Charles Gore, *Christ and Society,* p.18.
11. Baelz, Peter, *Perspective On Economics,* CIO, 1984, p.20.
12. Temple, William, *Religion And The Life Of Fellowship,* Longman, Green & Co, 1926, p.48.
13. Charles Elliott, *Praying The Kingdom,* Darton, Longman & Todd, 1985.
14. *Ibid*, p.20.
15. *Ibid*, p.55.
16. Charles Gore, *Christ And Society,* Allen and Unwin, 1928, pp.15–16.
17. *Ibid*, p.16

18. Denys Munby, "The Importance of Technical Competence" in *Essays In Anglican Self-Criticism*, edited David M. Paton, SCM, 1958.
19. *Ibid*, pp.57–58.
20. Paul Ramsey, *Who Speaks For The Church?*, The St Andrew Press, Edinburgh, p.138.
21. William Temple, "An Appeal To The Christian Conscience On The Subject Of Unemployment", *The Times*, 5 March 1934.
22. *Ibid*.
23. Neville Chamberlain, *The Times*, 10 March 1934.
24. *Ibid*.
25. William Temple, *Loc. cit*.
26. Neville Chamberlain, *The Times*, 10 March 1934.
27. *The Guardian*, 19 September 1986.
28. James Reston, *The New York Times*, 18 September 1985.
29. John Deedy, "The Moral Majority in Decline", *The Tablet*, 30 November 1985.
30. Peter Baelz, *Op. cit.*, p.14.

Chapter Eight

1. *Faith in the City. A call for action by church and nation*, Church House Publishing, 1985.
2. Norman Tebbit in a transcript from Channel 4 News, 3 December 1985.
3. R. H. Tawney, "Inaugural Lecture", *Poverty as an Industrial Problem*, William Morris Press, 1913.
4. For further details see G. F. A. Best, *Temporal Pillars*, Cambridge University Press, 1964.
5. General Synod *Report of Proceedings*, CIO, Vol.13, no.2, p.725.
6. South Africa: a factual memorandum, G. S. misc. 238, January 1986.
7. EIRIS brief, prepared for the July 1986 Synod and commissioned by the author.
8. *Ibid*.
9. The range of 15–17 is the result of the fact that the Commissioners publish only 8·7 per cent of their portfolio.
10. G. S. misc. 238, January 1986.
11. General Synod, *Report of Proceedings*, Vol.17, no.2, July 1986, p.542.
12. EIRIS brief prepared for the July 1986 Synod and commissioned by the author.
13. *Ibid*, p.10.
14. EIRIS letter to author (15 December 1986).
15. *Faith in the Facts.*, G. S. 529, 1982, pp.2–3.
16. Letter from Sir Douglas Lovelock to the Dean of St Paul's, dated 18 September 1986.

17. Letter from Andrew Phillips to Christian Concern for Southern Africa, 13 October 1986.
18. General Synod, *Op. cit.*, p.2.
19. *The Church and the Bomb,* Hodder & Stoughton and CIO, 1982.
20. *Ibid.*
21. *Ibid*, p.124.
22. *Ibid*, p.107.
23. *Ibid*, p.108.
24. *Ibid*
25. See, for example, Proverbs 8:22, Hebrews 1:1–3.
26. As to why both sets of parables must be read together, see Chapter 2.
27. *The Church and the Bomb,* p.106.
28. See Correlli Barnett, *The Audit of War,* Macmillan, 1986.
29. *The Church and the Bomb,* p.88.
30. *Ibid*, p.96.
31. *Ibid*, p.97.
32. *Ibid*, p.99.
33. Michael Ramsey, "Faith and Society" in *Durham Essays and Addresses,* SPCK, 1956, pp.41–2.
34. Lambeth Conference, 1978.
35. *The Church and the Bomb,* p.125.
36. Frank Longford, *The Bishops: a study of leaders in the Church today,* Sidgwick & Jackson, 1986, *p.86.*

Conclusion

1. Percy Widdrington, *The Return of Christendom,* Allen and Unwin, 1922.
2. Ronald Knox, *New Testament Commentary,* Vol.I, p.58, as quoted in A. M. Hunter, *Op. cit.*
3. See *Frederick Lewis Donaldson and the Christian Socialist Movement,* Barbara J. Butler, an unpublished M.Phil. thesis, University of Leeds, 1970.